PENGUIN BOOKS

STEALING BUDDHA'S DINNER

Bich Minh Nguyen (first name pronounced Bit) teaches literature and creative writing at Purdue University. She lives with her husband, the novelist Porter Shreve, in Chicago and West Lafayette, Indiana. *Stealing Buddha's Dinner*, her first book, was the recipient of the PEN/Jerard Fund Award. She is also the author of the novel *Short Girls*.

Praise for *Stealing Buddha's Dinner*

"A charming memoir . . . Her prose is engaging, precise, compact."
—*The New York Times Book Review*

"[D]eftly crafted . . . Far from being a memoir or what could be described as fitting into the kitschy ethnic-lit genre, her story is at once personal and broad, about one Vietnamese refugee navigating U.S. culture as well as an exploration of identity. . . . [S]he pays equal attention to the rhythm and poignancy of language to build her story as she does the circumstances into which she was born."
—*Los Angeles Times*

"Nguyen . . . succeeds as an author on many levels. She is a brave writer who is willing to share intimate family memories many of us would choose to keep secret. Her prose effortlessly pulls readers into her worlds. Her typical and not-so-typical childhood experiences give her story a universal flavor."
—*USA Today*

"Hilarious and poignant, her words will go straight to your heart."
—*Daily Candy*

"Nguyen brings back moments and sensations with such vivid clarity that readers will find themselves similarly jolted back in time. She's a sensuous writer—colors and textures weave together in her work to create a living fabric. This book should be bought and read anytime your soul hungers for bright language and close observation."
—*Star Tribune* (Minneapolis)

"It's the premise that makes the book relevant not only to anyone who's ever lusted after the perfect snack, but anyone who's ever felt different. Clever turns of phrase make Nguyen's book read quickly, and children of the '80s will be able to reminisce about pop culture along with her. The story resonates with anyone who's ever felt like an outsider."

—*San Francisco Chronicle*

"*Stealing Buddha's Dinner* is beautifully written. Nguyen . . . surely knows how to craft and shape sentences. She understands the evocative possibilities of language, is fearless in asserting the specificities of memories culled from early childhood and is, herself, an appealing character on the page. I believe Nguyen is a writer to watch, a tremendous talent with a gift for gorgeous sentences."

—*Chicago Tribune*

"The story of how one young girl could absorb all these cultural influences and assimilate drives *Stealing Buddha's Dinner* and Nguyen makes the journey both fiercely individual and universal."   —*Detroit Free Press*

"Nguyen is a gifted storyteller who doles out humor and hurt in equal portions. *Stealing Buddha's Dinner* [is] a tasty read. This memoir, which is also a tribute to 'all the bad [American] food, fashion, music, and hair of the deep 1980s,' feels vivid, true, and even nostalgic."

—*The Christian Science Monitor*

"[A] pungent, precisely captured memoir."   —*Elle*

"[Nguyen] makes the inability to fit in the springboard for a gracefully told remembrance that mixes the amusing and the touching to wonderful effect. She writes with Zen-like wisdom."   —*The Hartford Courant*

"The author's prose is lovely and her imagery fresh. And in her re-creation of a world populated by *Family Ties* [and] Ritz crackers . . . she has captured the 1980s with perfection. . . . This debut suggests she's a writer to watch."   —*Kirkus Reviews*

"'I came of age before ethnic was cool,' the author writes in her carefully crafted memoir of growing up in western Michigan as a Vietnamese refugee in the early 1980s. . . . What seems most to have caught her eye and fired her imagination, then as now, was food, which not only provides the title for each chapter of the memoir but also serves as a convenient shorthand for the cultural (and metaphorical) differences between Toll House cookies and green sticky rice cakes, between Pringles and *chao gio*, between American and Vietnamese. It's a clever device and—like the book itself—leaves the reader hungry for more."   —*Booklist*

Stealing Buddha's Dinner

a memoir

BICH MINH NGUYEN

PENGUIN BOOKS

PENGUIN BOOKS

Published by the Penguin Group

Penguin Group (USA) Inc., 375 Hudson Street, New York, New York 10014, U.S.A.

Penguin Group (Canada), 90 Eglinton Avenue East, Suite 700, Toronto,
Ontario, Canada M4P 2Y3 (a division of Pearson Penguin Canada Inc.)

Penguin Books Ltd, 80 Strand, London WC2R 0RL, England

Penguin Ireland, 25 St Stephen's Green, Dublin 2, Ireland (a division of Penguin Books Ltd)

Penguin Group (Australia), 250 Camberwell Road, Camberwell,
Victoria 3124, Australia (a division of Pearson Australia Group Pty Ltd)

Penguin Books India Pvt Ltd, 11 Community Centre,
Panchsheel Park, New Delhi – 110 017, India

Penguin Group (NZ), 67 Apollo Drive, Rosedale, North Shore 0632,
New Zealand (a division of Pearson New Zealand Ltd)

Penguin Books (South Africa) (Pty) Ltd, 24 Sturdee Avenue,
Rosebank, Johannesburg 2196, South Africa

Penguin Books Ltd, Registered Offices: 80 Strand, London WC2R 0RL, England

First published in the United States of America by Viking Penguin,
a member of Penguin Group (USA) Inc. 2007
Published in Penguin Books 2008

10   9   8

Copyright © Bich Minh Nguyen, 2007
All rights reserved

Portions of this book were published as the selections "A World Without Measurements" in *Gourmet;*
"Toadstools" in *Dream Me Home Safely: Writers on Growing Up in America,* edited by Susan Richards
Shreve (Houghton Mifflin, 2003); and "The Good Immigrant Student" in *Tales Out of School: Contemporary Writers on Their Student Years,* edited by Susan Richards Shreve and Porter Shreve (Beacon Press,
2001).

THE LIBRARY OF CONGRESS HAS CATALOGED THE HARDCOVER EDITION AS FOLLOWS:
Nguyen, Bich Minh.
     Stealing Buddha's dinner : a memoir / Bich Minh Nguyen.
        p.   cm.
     ISBN 978-0-670-03832-9 (hc.)
     ISBN 978-0-14-311303-4 (pbk.)
     1. Nguyen, Bich Minh—Childhood and youth.   2. Immigrants—Michigan—Grand Rapids—
Biography.   3. Vietnamese Americans—Michigan—Grand Rapids—Biography.   4. Americans—
Food.   5. Grand Rapids (Mich.)—Biography.   I. Title.
     CT275.N523A3   2007
     977.4'5600495922092—dc22   2006047219
     [B]

Printed in the United States of America
Set in Adobe Caslon with Goudy Sans
Designed by Daniel Lagin

for my family

Contents

Stealing Buddha's Dinner

1

Pringles

WE ARRIVED IN GRAND RAPIDS WITH FIVE DOLLARS and a knapsack of clothes. Mr. Heidenga, our sponsor, set us up with a rental house, some groceries—boxed rice, egg noodles, cans of green beans—and gave us dresses his daughters had outgrown. He hired my father to work a filling machine at North American Feather. Mr. Heidenga wore wide sport coats and had yellow hair. My sister and I were taught to say his name in a hushed tone to show respect. But if he stopped by to check on us my grandmother would tell us to be silent because that was part of being good. *Hello, girls,* he would say, stooping to pat us on the head.

It was July 1975, but we were cold. Always cold, after Vietnam, and my uncle Chu Cuong rashly spent two family dollars on a jacket from the Salvation Army, earning my grandmother's scorn. For there were seven of us to feed in that gray house on Baldwin Street: my father, Grandmother Noi, Uncles Chu Cuong, Chu Anh, and Chu Dai (who wasn't really an uncle but Cuong's best friend), and my sister and me. Upstairs belonged to the uncles, and downstairs my sister and I shared a room with Noi. My father did not know how to sleep through the night. He paced around the house, double-checking the lock on the front door; he glanced sideways out the taped-up windows, in case someone was watching from the street. When at last he settled down on the living room sofa, a tweedy green relic from Mr. Heidenga's basement, he kept one hand on the sword he had bought from a pawnshop with his second paycheck. My father had showed my sister and me the spiral carvings on the handle. He turned the sword slowly, its dull metal almost gleaming, and let us feel the weight of the blade.

On Baldwin Street all of the houses were porched and lopsided, missing slats and posts like teeth knocked out of a sad face. Great heaps of rusted cars lined the curbs, along with beer bottles that sparkled in any hint of sunlight. I spent a lot of time staring at the street, waiting for something to happen or someone to appear. Chu Anh got a job working second shift at a tool and die plant, and sometimes he and my father would meet each other on the street, coming and going from the bus stop.

My sister was also named Anh, but with an accent no one pronounces anymore. A year older than I, she was the ruler of all our toys. We amassed a closet full of them, thanks to the bins at our sponsor's church. We had so much, we became reckless. We threw Slinkies until they tangled and drowned paper dolls. Someone gave us tricycles and we traveled the house relentlessly, forgetting our uncles sleeping upstairs. We didn't know that they had to get up in the middle of the night, or that our father competed for pillows and comforters from the reject pile at work. We didn't know that we were among the lucky.

I remember bare feet on old wood floors; shivering after a bath. Noi knitted heavy sweaters from marled-colored rayon my father bought at Kmart. Puffs of steam rose from the kitchen stove where she cooked our daily rice. One blizzard morning, Noi let my sister and me run outside in our pajamas and fuzzy slippers. The snow fell on my face and for a moment I laughed and waved. Then a gust of wind sent me tumbling into a snowbank and I screamed so much, Noi thought the weather had turned into an attack. She snatched us up and ran inside.

We had been living on Baldwin Street for almost a year when Mr. Heidenga invited us to dinner at his family's massive, pillared house in East Grand Rapids. The Heidengas had a cook, like Alice on *The Brady Bunch,* and she must have fed us—me, my sister Anh, and the Heidenga daughters, all sequestered together in the kitchen. But I don't remember eating anything. I only remember staring, and silence, and Heather Heidenga— who might have been Marcia, with that oval face—opening a canister of Pringles. Anh and I were transfixed by the bright red cylinder and the mustache grin on Mr. Pringles's broad, pale face. The Heidenga girl pried off the top and crammed a handful of chips into her mouth. We watched the crumbs fall from her fingers to the floor.

Mrs. Heidenga swished into the kitchen to see how we were doing. Later, my father would swear that she served them raw hamburgers for dinner. Mrs. Heidenga was tall and blond, glamorous in a pastel pantsuit and clicking heels. When she touched her daughters' hair her bracelets clattered richly. Nicole Heidenga, who was younger than her sister but older than mine, waited for her mother to go back to the dining room. She shoved her hand into the can of Pringles and said, "Where's your mom?"

Anh and I made no answer. We had none to give.

We had left Vietnam in the spring of 1975, when my sister was two and I was eight months old. By then, everyone in Saigon knew the war was lost, and to stay meant being sent to reeducation camps, or worse. The neighbors spoke of executions and what the Communists would do to their children; they talked of people vanished and tortured—a haunting reminder of what my grandfather had endured in the North. My father heard that some Americans were going to airlift children out of the country, and he wondered if he could get Anh and me on one of those planes. Operation Babylift it was called, and over the course of April would carry away two thousand children. But on April 4 the first flight crashed at the Tan Son Nhut air base, killing most on board. My father decided he had to find another way, though time was running out for Saigon. Americans were fleeing. Wealthy Vietnamese worked bribes to get any route out. Masses of would-be refugees mobbed the airport.

On the morning of April 29 the last helicopters rose from the roofs of the American Embassy. The North Vietnamese were closing in, firing rockets at the downtown neighborhoods, where looters were still smashing in windows. Tanks would be rolling into the presidential palace by the next day. Chu Cuong, who was based at the naval headquarters, called Chu Anh at the army communications center. Two dozen ships had been waiting at the Saigon River for the past month, preparing for the end. Now it was time. *I'm getting on a ship,* Chu Cuong said. *You get the family on any one you can. Go now.*

He had been to the United States for training missions—there's a photograph of him confident and grinning in hip-slung bell-bottoms, his hair windblown while the Statue of Liberty rises up behind him—and he was certain that we would all be able to meet up there. *We'll find each other,* he said casually, as if America were a small town.

Chu Anh went straight home and sat down, dazed. He was known as the level-headed practical one, and he wasn't so prepared to abandon everything and throw our fate into an old Vietnamese warship. My father argued with him. *There's no other way,* he pointed out. *This is our last chance.*

We headed toward the Vietnamese naval headquarters, Chu Anh driving a motorbike while holding Anh in one arm, and my father on his own bike, with Noi on the back holding fast to me. They drove through the twenty-four-hour curfew and the thundering of shells. All around us people were running, dropping suitcases and clothes, trying to flag down cars.

At the Saigon River my father and uncle abandoned their once fiercely protected bikes only to see thousands of people already gathered at the headquarters gates, where guards patrolled with automatic rifles. They began searching for another way to the docks, pushing through the screaming crowd. A full panic had hit the city, the kind that sent people racing after airplanes on the runway, that made people offer their babies to departing American soldiers.

It was almost dusk—no lights came on—by the time my

father spied a passageway blocked by a roll of barbed wire. He motioned to Chu Anh, who still wore his soldier's boots, to step down on the wire so the rest of the family could get past it. How this happened—quickly, almost easily—my father doesn't understand. Had no one else seen the passage? Did no one see us go? Sometimes, he says, he dreams it didn't happen at all.

As we ran to the docks a guard grabbed my father and swung him around, pushing the barrel of an M-16 at his stomach. *What are you doing here? Go back,* he ordered.

My father just looked at him. Chu Anh and Noi were moving ahead with me and Anh. *Shoot me if you have to,* he said. *But my family is going.* He backed away, turning to run. The guard didn't shoot.

Most of the ships were already gone. The river was filling up with rowboats and dinghies, whatever means people could find. We climbed onto one of the last ships in line, using a ladder that someone pulled up the second my father touched the deck.

We left that night out of luck, drive, fear pushed into fearlessness. And by further luck the ship inched forward down the long river, everyone holding their breath for the gunfire they expected but which never came. As we reached the ocean the U.S. Seventh Fleet appeared in the distance to guide us toward the Philippines.

Those days on the ship, people jostled each other to keep the small space they had claimed among the thousand or so on board. There was not enough rice or fresh water, and all around us children screamed and wailed without stopping. My father says that my sister and I did not cry the entire trip, and I'd like to believe it. I'd like to think we gave them something—a little peace, maybe. My father, uncle, and grandmother didn't talk much, worrying about Chu Cuong, if he had made it out safely, where he was at that moment. One morning, the word *apples* swept around the ship. My father hurried to collect our family's portion and brought back half an apple for Noi. She fed it to my sister and me, taking none for herself.

Then another word: *fire.* Somewhere belowdecks one had started in a room near the ammunitions hold. *This ship is going to blow up,* someone said. In the rising hysteria my father, grandmother, and uncle quietly sat down with Anh and me, preparing to accept whatever would happen. They waited. But the ship stayed on course. Below, workers had managed to extinguish the fire.

Late at night my father slipped away from the deck and made friends with the crewmen. He had always been a charmer, the popular kid surrounded by friends, the smooth talker who could dance any woman around the room. Now he worked his way into the kitchen and struck a deal with one of the cooks, listening to the guy's long stories of home and teaching him how to play poker in exchange for a little powdered milk for my sister and me.

At Subic Bay in the Philippines we transferred to a U.S. ship headed for Guam. There, at a refugee camp, we awaited entry papers into the United States. For the next month my father looked for anyone he might know from his neighborhood in Saigon. He joined groups of boys who dared each other to climb the skinny, arching coconut trees and knock down the fruit. It was a small risk for some flavor, a taste that would remind them of home.

One day, a couple of weeks into the waiting, my father got into the usual long line for rice and noticed a man, far ahead, wearing yellow pants. They were brighter than the day, tinged with chartreuse in a lava-lamp pattern, and the man was standing a little outside the line, his left leg askance as if striking a pose.

My father recognized those pants. They were his own, a favorite pair, ones he had often worn when he went out at night.

My father stepped out of the line and walked toward the man in the yellow pants, who turned around. It was Chu Cuong. He had been in the camp all this time, wondering if the family had been able to get on a ship. He had worn the pants every day, always making sure to stand a little apart from everyone else, just in case. He was glad, he said, that he wouldn't have to wear those pants all over America, looking for us.

From Guam we flew to Arkansas and the refugee camp at Fort Chaffee. We were in America at last, but there was little to tell from behind the barbed-wire, chain-link fence. There were no trees to climb, and not a coconut in sight. The days strung themselves into months of waiting: standing in meal lines; playing cards; hoping for sponsors; sitting around the tents and barracks talking about what they had heard America was like. The optimists said *easy money, fast cars, girls with blue eyes;* others said *cold, filled with crazy people.* My father and uncles traded English words for cigarettes. Chu Anh in particular knew more than most; he'd always excelled at school and had gotten in two years of college before he'd had to join the army.

My father made friends with one of the American soldiers guarding the camp and brought back a few bars of chocolate for Noi. She spent her time minding my sister and me and talking to women who spent their hours crying, longing to go back home. Later, a group of Vietnamese in the camp organized a campaign to get sent back to Saigon. They were fools, my father said, and did they think they would return to a better life in Vietnam, greeted by the North Vietnamese? Even he, an impatient man, knew all he could do was wait to see which city we would be given. Only after we left Fort Chaffee did he realize how much time he had wasted in the camp. He had felt almost safe there among his fellow Vietnamese. He had forgotten to think ahead, imagine us living among white people who spoke only English and looked at us strangely. He had forgotten to prepare.

Every afternoon my father went to look at the names posted at the camp's central office. When at last our Nguyen appeared, buried in the list of Nguyens, my father brought back three options: sponsors in California, Wyoming, and Michigan. To make such a swift decision with little information to go on, my family relied on vague impressions volunteered by friends of friends in the camp; they relied on rumors. California: warm but had the most lunatics. Wyoming: cowboys. Michigan was the blank unknown. My father would have chosen California, where he heard many other Vietnamese were going. But my grandmother, the head of the family, hesitated. Back in Saigon, she had met a woman whose son had studied at the University of Michigan on a scholarship. Such a possibility had grown in her mind until it became near legend, too symbolic to refuse. And here it was right in front of her.

The night before we left for Grand Rapids my father and uncles pooled their money—thirty-five dollars—to throw a party for their friends who were still waiting for sponsors. They had only five dollars remaining after buying beer and cigarettes but figured, so be it. They wanted a proper farewell to the people who knew them, and to toast the lives they had foregone. *We are people without a country,* someone in the camp said. *Until we walk out of that gate,* my father replied. *And then we are American.*

I came of age in the 1980s, before *diversity* and *multicultural awareness* trickled into western Michigan. Before ethnic was cool. Before Thai restaurants became staples in every town. When I think of Grand Rapids I remember city signs covered in images of rippling flags, proclaiming "An All-American City." A giant billboard looming over the downtown freeway boasted the slogan to all who drove the three-lane S-curve. As a kid, I couldn't figure out what "All-American" was supposed to mean. Was it a promise, a threat, a warning?

Of the two hundred thousand people who populate Grand Rapids, the majority are Dutch descendants, Christian Reformed, conservative. My family was among the several thousand Vietnamese refugees brought to the area, mostly through churches participating in the federal resettlement effort. My father and uncles and grandmother were grateful for a place to go—how could they be anything less?—and preferred to overlook how the welcoming smile of our sponsor gave way to a scowling face behind a drugstore cash register: *Don't you people know how to speak English? Why don't you go back to where you came from?*

Grand Rapids brings to mind Gerald Ford, office furniture, and Amway, created here in 1959 by Richard DeVos and Jay Van Andel. The company is now headquartered just east of the city in the town of Ada. My stepmother Rosa, whom my father married in 1979, would one day move us there in an effort to keep our family together. DeVos and Van Andel have poured millions of dollars into Grand Rapids and the Republican Party. Their names are emblazoned everywhere on buildings and in the *Grand Rapids Press,* a reminder of what and whom the town represents, as if the sea of blond—so much I could swear I was dreaming in wheat—could let a foreigner forget. In school hallways blond heads glided, illuminated in the lockers creaking open and slamming shut, taunting me to be what I only wished I could be. That was the dilemma, the push and pull. The voice saying, *Come on in. Now transform. And if you cannot, then disappear.*

In 1983 the construction of the Amway Grand Plaza Hotel's glass tower marked the city's first skyscraper, reaching twenty-nine stories. I remember the breathless chronicle of the building in the newspaper, and the opening of restaurants too fancy to dare consider. It would be years before I stepped foot inside the velvet green lobby, years before my father and stepmother ate an anniversary dinner—the only one I ever knew them to celebrate—at the 1913 Restaurant, where they ate chocolate mousse that arrived in an edible shell that cracked open when they tapped it. When I drive Highway 131 skirting downtown, I can't help seeing pride and forlornness in the mirrored obelisk of the Grand Plaza jutting up from the landscape of brick buildings left over from the nineteenth century furniture boom. The Grand River cuts through the city on its way to Lake Michigan, a swath for salmon and waste, a gleaming opacity beneath the lit-up bridges at night.

My family ventured into downtown only a few times a year, for the Festival of the Arts (known simply as Festival), the Hispanic Festival where Rosa volunteered, Fourth of July fireworks, and the city's Celebration on the Grand. Crowds of families would set up blankets and lawn chairs on the Indian mounds at Ah-Nab-Awen Park, waiting for fireworks to rain over the river. We'd hurry to join them, my father's mood darkening as he drove around for a parking space, circling the elephantine Calder sculpture that anchors the downtown business area. I had love-hate feelings for the Calder: it represented Grand Rapids, being part of the city's logo, yet it was also real art—something greater than the ordinary life I knew.

Throughout my childhood I wondered, so often it became a buzzing dullness, why we had ended up here, and why we couldn't leave. I would stare at a map of the United States and imagine us in New York or Boston or Los Angeles. I had no idea what such cities were like, but I was convinced people were happier out on the coasts, living in a nexus between so much land and water. Gazing at the crisscrossing lines of Manhattan or the blue vastness of the oceans, I would feel something I could only describe as missingness.

In the town of Holland, about half an hour's drive from Grand Rapids, the annual spring Tulip Time Festival brings all other activities to a halt. The citizenry work double-time to get their front-yard tulips in order. There are contests, prizes, prestige to be had. There's a parade. People line up early with their lawn chairs to wait for girls in braids and wooden clogs to come clopping down the streets.

Once, in second grade, a substitute teacher gave a geography lesson by asking students to name the places they wanted to visit. She had a large globe beside her, spinning it absently as she talked.

I was the first student she called on. Tongue-tied by shyness, I couldn't think of what to say. "Holland," I blurted out.

Brightly the teacher said, "Here or overseas?"

I must have stared at her dumbly, for she repeated the question, "This Holland or the one overseas?" Perhaps she thought I didn't understand. But I was amazed that of all the places in the world, she thought that I would choose the town of Holland. Wasn't it enough that I would choose the country?

"Not here," I said. "Not this one."

In 1975 we were new in America and two years away from the arrival of Rosa. Before she swept us up and out of Baldwin Street, we lived in a house of splintery wooden floors that slanted in different directions. We huddled close as if in a cave. Our Vietnamese mixed with the American voices rising from the old television my father had brought back to life. Our cave had feather smells and rice smells, tricycles in the house, bare feet. My sister and I played all day in our pajamas, even going outside in them, though no farther than the curb so our grandmother could watch us from the porch. In the cave we ate spring rolls and drank 7UP, tore open packages of licorice and Wrigley's spearmint gum. My sister and I fell asleep with plastic phones and floppy dolls from the bins at Blessed Christian Reformed Church. We held on to oranges and plums, desserts from Noi, saved so long we forgot to eat them.

When Christmas rolled around we had a genuine fake tree with lights and a star. Anh and I had no idea what the word *Christmas* meant; to us it was, and remained for years, glitter and gifts. We had to put together the pieces of America that came to us through television, song lyrics, Meijer Thrifty Acres, and our father, coming home from work each day with a new kind of candy in his pocket. We couldn't get enough Luden's wild-cherry-flavored cough drops, or Pringles stacked in their shiny red canister, a mille-feuille of promises. My father's mustache was nothing like Mr. Pringles's, which winged out jauntily. Mr. Pringles was like Santa Claus or Mr. Heidenga—a big white man, gentle of manner, whose face signaled a bounty of provisions.

So we hoarded our Pringles cans, rolling them on the floor, making them into piggy banks with pennies donated by our uncles. The Pringles glowed by window light, their fine curvatures nearly translucent. So delicate, breaking into salty shards on our tongues. These were blissful days, or so they seemed to me. I did not know we were poor, or refugees, or that we had been born in another hemisphere. I didn't know that a kind of apprehension gathered around my father each evening, making him check the corners of every room, the spaces behind open doors. I wonder what he thought about—he doesn't say, can't remember. Did he wake up gasping with shock, gripping the sword, forgetting where he was? Did he dream of Saigon? Did he think ahead to what he would have to tell my sister and me, one day, if we asked about our mother? How would he explain the choice he had had to make?

Back in the chill of the rental house that cost one hundred precious dollars a month, the only future he could see lay in work, in whirls of processed feathers. For the beauty of a Pringle could only go so far, and must be paid for. My uncles felt it, too. When they slept all day after working all night, or played the same melancholy Simon & Garfunkel song over and over, my grandmother told me not to bother them with questions about what all the words meant.

Too much to ask, and too much to do. English to learn, streets to navigate, work to manage, food to buy, friends to find. And so my father and uncles and grandmother rose, always in darkness, toward this new life.

2

Forbidden Fruit

WHEN MY FATHER WORKED AT THE NORTH AMERICAN Feather Company he always came home with down in his hair, a fine scattering like the Michigan snow that seemed to fall without stopping those first winters in America. When he tossed me into the air to make me laugh he smelled like factory feathers and old brass. The scent lingered even when the days began to brighten, the gray cloud cover over Grand Rapids slowly lifting.

My father made fast friends with the other Vietnamese refugees who had landed in Grand Rapids. They cobbled together seeds and ingredients, information on weather and how to send letters to family in Vietnam. Some people drove across the state to Canada, where Chinese groceries in Windsor sold real jasmine rice, lemongrass, and the fleshy, familiar fruits that had no English translation. Now Noi could plant cilantro, mint, *ram rau*. She grew more at ease in our neighborhood and started taking my sister and me to a nearby park. We never saw any other children around. Shielded by "Beware of Dog" signs, the other houses looked empty, shut tight against us. Still, Noi fixed our hair in side ponytails and dressed us in corduroy jumpers that came in a grocery bag from Mr. Heidenga's daughters. She stood sedately, watching us play on the jungle gym and swings. Under her puffy nylon jacket from Goodwill she wore the jade green *ao dai* she had sewn.

On good days, when he was in a happy mood, my father let us walk with him to Meijer to get groceries and choose any kind of candy we wanted. So we introduced ourselves to Smarties, Hershey's chocolate bars, candy necklaces, and pink-tipped candy cigarettes. On summer days Noi took us to the farmers' market. Anh and I held hands as we trailed her, looking up at the canvas canopy and the swaying silver scales. Noi bargained wordlessly, pulling dollar bills from a little lacquer purse with a wooden handle. Her arms filled with brown sacks. At home she would unveil grapes and nectarines, tomatoes and greens, taut bulbs of onion.

The allure of the fruits—their roundness, aliveness—enchanted my sister and me, but the choicest pieces went first to a plate that lay before the golden statue of Buddha in the living room. This was the altar for him and for our dead relatives, to whom my grandmother paid respect every morning and evening. My father had built a shelf for the Buddha, who sat perpetually smooth, peaceful, eyes closed, his palms facing up. The fruit made a solemn offering, and for two whole days, sometimes longer, it had to remain there untouched between Noi's candles and stems of incense. I was in awe of this process. Did Buddha and the ancestors know the fruit was there for the taking? Did they prefer apples or bananas or plums? Once in a great while Noi put an entire pineapple on the altar and I wondered how they would eat it. I always expected the fruit to disappear, and when it did not I marveled at the ancestors' lack of hunger, their self-control.

I tried to work up the nerve to pluck off just one grape, but I feared my dead relatives would tell on me. Buddha might snap open his eyes and let my grandmother know that his food had been disrespected. The thought kept me at bay, circling the altar like a nighttime prowler. The fruit might as well have been protected behind glass, the dusty grapes turning into jewels.

When at last Noi took up two pieces of fruit for my sister and me—peaches and plums in the summer, apples and pears in the fall, oranges in winter—we held on to them like lifeboats. We kept them in our laps, smoothing the varnish of the apples until they bruised, cradling the mottled green pears in our arms. We loved to sniff peaches, tickling our faces with their fuzz. Hours would pass like this, our admiration steady, our anticipation covering the afternoons. At last Noi would pull the fruit away from us and carve them into wedges—plums were the only fruit we ate with the skins still on. We could never get enough. The fruit seemed dearer to us than candy, and I believed that the transformation from globe to glistening slices involved some kind of magic. It would be years before either my sister or I ever bit into a whole apple.

Later, Noi found pomegranates, mangoes, persimmons, and coconuts at the newly opened Saigon Market. All of these were set upon the altar before making their way to our mouths, and it was a lesson in patience and desire. We were eating gifts every time.

On the New Year's Eve between 1977 and 1978 my father and Uncle Chu Anh were hanging out in a rec room of an apartment complex off East Beltline. It was a Vietnamese party, everyone dancing to Donna Summer and Debby Boone and sharing bottles of Martini & Rossi Asti Spumante. My father was sitting at a table with a group of guys and a pack of cards when he saw two women pausing at the doorway. One had curly black hair, and it took him a moment to realize that she wasn't Vietnamese. But she didn't look white, either. "Look at that," one of the guys said with a low whistle.

The two women were Rosa, a second-generation Mexican-American, and Shirley, a daughter of German-Jewish immigrants by way of the Dominican Republic. They had become friends while teaching ESL classes in downtown Grand Rapids, and had been invited to the party by a Vietnamese guy Shirley had met at the community education center. My father didn't waste time. He got to Rosa first, asking her to dance to what happened to be one of her favorite songs, "You Light Up My Life." Shirley fell into step with Chu Anh, and together the four of them drew the stares of the crowd. I wonder if my father was wearing his favorite olive-patterned shirt, collars set wide against the tawny lapels of his one sport jacket. Maybe Rosa wore a mauve-colored chiffon dress, puffed at the shoulder and tight at the wrists, that floated out when my father, an expert dancer, twirled her around the room. I wonder if he saw in her face a familiar expression of unease, of knowing what it was to live in this pale city in which they had ended up, by chance, by way of survival.

After a while he suggested they ditch the party and go get something to eat. Rosa agreed, but when they walked out into the freezing air he realized he had no idea where to go. So he took her to the only restaurant he could think of, the one in the lobby of the Holiday Inn. Mr. Heidenga had put us up in this same hotel our first few nights in Michigan, while he found us a place to live. Meal after meal my grandmother had requested plain bowls of the white rice she craved. The cook didn't know how to make it, and Noi longed to go back into the kitchen and fix it herself. My sister remembers restlessness, a vague feeling of expectation. She remembers my father ordering us as much tapioca pudding as we wanted.

My father and Rosa do not remember what they talked about that New Year's Eve, but something between them was decided that night. Soon, Rosa would be standing in our house on Baldwin, laughing at the fruit on the altar. It belonged in the kitchen, she said, not the living room. She picked up an orange from the altar and Noi shook her head. Without English to explain, my grandmother gently pulled the fruit out of Rosa's hand and set it back on its plate. Rosa understood then. "It's your custom," she would say later, year after year, Tet after Tet. "It's the way Vietnamese do things."

She roamed through the house, looking through the cupboards to see what we ate, surveying the room that Anh and I shared with Noi. We slept in a rattling steel-framed bunk bed that had come with the house—Noi on the top bunk, Anh and I on the bottom. At dinner Rosa sat down at the kitchen table with us and ate Noi's *pho,* trying to pick up the slippery noodles with her chopsticks. They splashed back into the broth until Rosa cut them with a spoon against the side of the bowl. Rosa had a large chest, bigger than any I'd seen even on television, and when she leaned over to eat I caught my first real-life glimpse of a woman's cleavage.

After we ate, Anh and I ran back to our living room domain to watch television. It was a black and white, with antennae sprouting out and covered in tinfoil. Upstairs, my uncles played records on the hi-fi they'd saved up to buy. They could listen to the Carpenters, the Eagles, and Paul Simon until the grooves wore out. Anh and I divided our time among toys, television, and our uncles' songs. We learned English this way, matching sound with word with meaning. *Why do birds suddenly appear every time you are near?* We watched *Wonder Woman, Police Woman, Happy Days,* and *Sesame Street.* We sat close to the screen, shouting out dialogue and names. My favorite actress was Angie Dickinson, whose name seemed to match her flowing hair and tough, sassy work patrolling the streets.

I could feel Rosa watching us, her eyes taking in the scratched floors, the Salvation Army furniture, the wooden clock carved into the shape of Vietnam—the only decoration on the living room wall. Anh and I sat together in our beloved green chair and Noi brought us one apple each. We held them carefully, saving them, always saving them, while we switched from Bert and Ernie to Fat Albert.

Rosa brought us groceries and gifts—milk and mittens for Anh and me, shampoo and toothpaste, *National Geographic*s for the uncles. She ate whatever Noi cooked, impressing us all with her effort to master chopsticks. She slid right into our lives. After dinner, she said that children should not be riding tricycles around the house. Those belonged outside. She asked us to please tidy up our toys. She said we shouldn't be eating so much candy. Then one day she approached us while we were in the bathtub. Noi's method was to scrub us down with a washcloth until we turned pink. She had been washing our hair with soap and Rosa tried to communicate with her that shampoo—a yellow bottle of Johnson & Johnson—would be better. Anh and I screamed with terror, hating the cold liquid on our scalps, until Rosa showed us the foamy bubbles and how they floated on the water. "See?" she said, one of the things she was always saying, as if she were literally opening our eyes.

Rosa had been dating my father for about two months when she started talking about how Anh would be five years old in March and we had to have a party. I remember sitting at the Formica table in the kitchen while Rosa washed dishes, explaining to me what birthdays were. In August, she said, I would be four years old. Rosa said that in America everyone had birthdays. She described them in terms of Christmas and Tet, with presents and food and more presents. This sounded like a windfall, especially coming so soon after the money pleasures and moon cakes of Tet.

All of my legal records—from my original *permanent resident alien* card to my citizenship papers and driver's license—list a birthday I don't celebrate. Perhaps because his mind was distracted, or perhaps because in Vietnam death is remembered more than birthdays, my father forgot our birth dates when he had to write them down at the refugee camp in Guam. So he guessed. It was years before he and Noi agreed on the more likely days (sometime in early March for Anh, late August for me). Noi said what mattered was the year: Anh, born in the year of the buffalo, and I in the year of the tiger. *El tigre,* Rosa would say with a *rrrr*-ing sound whenever she caught me in a sour mood.

The first birthday cake I ever saw was from the Meijer bakery. It was oblong, covered in rosettes and pink and white frosting, a vision of wealth and excess. The sugar flowers quickened my heartbeat, hinting at a whole new concept of sweetness. A giant candle, shaped in the number five, sat in the middle of the cake, and Anh in her new red velveteen dress smiled for Rosa's camera. She and my father had invited people I had never seen before, mostly friends of my father's who wore their hand-sewn *ao dai*s and best thrift store suits. The brightly wrapped gifts piled up around Anh. She discovered, to her dismay, that a few of the presents were for me, because our fair-minded father had insisted that gifts had to be given to both of us. This realization hit my sister hard. It may have been her first true American moment: she cried, stamped her foot, and shrieked angrily that it was *her* birthday and I shouldn't be getting a thing.

Not long after, Rosa introduced us to her daughter, Crissy. She was eight, four and a half years older than I, pretty and petulant, her hands stuffed into the pockets of her denim jumper. She frowned and scrunched up her freckled nose. I was probably too young to be startled by the news of Crissy's sudden existence, but she wasn't too young to be upset about ours. *Pissed off* was one of the first phrases she taught me, followed by its fond abbreviation, *P.O.'ed. I'm really P.O.'ed*, she would say. What's that? I'd ask. *Pissed off*. What does that mean? *P.O.'ed.*

It had always been just the two of them, Rosa and Crissy, in their Dutch Colonial apartment complex north of downtown. Now Rosa brought her daughter to the house on Baldwin Street and instructed us to play together. Crissy only warmed up to us when my father gave us an extra-large supply of Pringles and Hershey bars. She tantalized us with swear words, doling out only *damn* and *hell*, promising much better ones if she felt like telling. She taught us to race from the living room and jump onto the top of the bunk bed. Crissy and Anh could do this with ease, but on one of my failed tries I gashed my leg open on a piece of metal sticking out from the bed. I have no recollection of pain from that long bloody cut, but I do remember sitting in the living room with my grandmother's pillow, leg propped up while I sipped my own treasured bottle of 7UP. The scar on my leg remains, barely faded, a reminder of the force with which Crissy and Rosa burst into our lives.

That fall, Rosa, whom Anh and I had been instructed to call Mom, moved all of us away from Baldwin to a house on Florence Street, on the southeast side of town. And in January, just a little over a year after they had met, my father and Rosa, seven months' pregnant with my brother Vinh, married at the courthouse in downtown Grand Rapids. So much snow fell that day that the roads grew impassable, and no one could make it to the house for the small wedding reception. Months later, Chu Anh and Shirley would also get married. In my green patchwork dress that exactly matched my sister's, I would eat the maraschino cherries from my Shirley Temples and watch Chu Anh and Shirley dance in the Holiday Inn's ballroom.

Our house on Florence Street was surrounded by similar ranches and split-levels. It had army-green vinyl siding, a narrow garage, and a blue front door with three diamond-shaped windows. Set into a hill, the house looked like a flat ranch from the front but exposed the basement in the back. A few years after we moved in, my father and Rosa had an addition built onto it. On the top floor my father cut a space for a doorway leading to a deck that he never got around to building. The door remains there still, threatening to open out onto nothing.

Anh, Crissy, and I shared a bedroom that had pear-green

carpet patterned into almost-paisleys. Anh and I had another bunk bed, this one painted white, and I got the top bunk. That small space between bed and ceiling soon became my only privacy, filled with overdue library books. My sisters dominated every other spot in the room and I accepted this, already knowing that my role was to be out of the way, apart and observing. Living on Florence Street made me more aware of my footsteps and my voice—more aware of the construct of family. I knew, for instance, that it was strange that Crissy didn't have a father, but I also knew better than to press anyone about it. My father and Rosa had in common a deadly stare, part frown, part rage, when they were met with talk they didn't like, and this look always earned my silence. There were so many things that could never be spoken. Whenever one of us kids asked Rosa a question she didn't want to answer, she'd reply, "Be quiet" or "It's none of your business." My father would just emit a grunting noise. Almost any question—from whether we could go see a movie to why all of Rosa's family lived forty minutes away in a town called Fruitport—could yield such responses.

My father set up the Buddha and ancestor altar not in the living room but in Noi's room, which lay across the hall from me, Anh, and Crissy. Buddha's shift in place was one of many adjustments for me. No longer would Rosa tolerate tricycles in the house at any time. Our toy closet was no more. Rosa taught us how to make our beds and put clothes in dresser drawers. She drew up a list of chores and said we would have to take turns washing dishes. She checked on us while we brushed our teeth, to make sure we actually did it. I preferred Noi's method, which was simply to ask, *"Dang rang?"* The simple phrase—*Did you brush your teeth?*—carried a trill and a rhyme, somehow making the task a little less awful. Now the rules of the house were governed not by my grandmother but by my new stepmother.

Uncle Chu Cuong and his friend Chu Dai, who had lived with us since our days in the refugee camps, were gloriously exempt, free and easy bachelors. They lived in the basement, which the previous owners had supplied with a padded wet bar and shiny silver wallpaper. Chu Dai plugged in the hi-fi and let music rise up the stairs. They always played my favorite, "50 Ways to Leave Your Lover," knowing how much I liked to repeat the rhymes. *Slip out the back, Jack. Make a new plan, Stan. Hop on the bus, Gus.* I pictured guys as carefree as my uncles, elusive, unpinnable. Chu Cuong and Chu Dai were making good money at a jewelry plant, enough to buy all the records they wanted, plus a sage-green Chevy Maverick and a motorcycle.

Chu Anh was away at school. The year before, he had confessed to my father that he couldn't take another moment working at the tool and die plant. He longed to go to college, he said. Chu Anh had always loved studying, and had trained to be an aeronautical engineer in Vietnam. "So go," my father said.

"What about the family?" Chu Anh had asked, thinking about tuition, loans, groceries.

"Don't worry," my father said. "I'm not going anywhere."

Chu Anh enrolled in nearby Calvin College, but when he realized its Christian Reformed affiliation was serious he applied for a transfer to the University of Michigan, located two hours away. Few things ever made my grandmother happier, and she cherished the photograph he sent home from Ann Arbor: Chu Anh standing near a snowdrift on campus, carrying a bundle of engineering books and wearing a light sweater, hipster pants, and steel-gray glasses. Such evidence made it easier to let another one of her sons go.

My father had been promoted to better hours and machinery at North American Feather, though he still came home smelling of dust, his hair speckled white. On weekends off, he worked on his 1972 pewter-gray Mustang, which had a black vinyl interior that scorched the skin on summer days. He had bought it not long before his fateful New Year's Eve date with Rosa. He loved to drive around by himself, visiting friends who lived in Wyoming and Caledonia. He began shopping the secondhand stores more carefully. But nothing ever replaced that favorite shirt, shiny with a flaring collar, patterned all over with what looked like green olives stuffed with pimento. My father wore it whenever he went out wanting to look "sharp." It was a word Rosa introduced to our vocabulary. "Lookin' good!" she would croon. "Man, that is *sharp*." It's startling to see how fresh and happy they were in those early photographs—a late seventies couple with shaggy hair, boho hems, and big, dazed grins on their faces.

Outside, the hill in our yard was just steep enough for decent sledding, and the previous owners had left their swing set. Noi had plenty of space for a garden, and in the early morning she fed pieces of stale bread to the squirrels who approached without fear and ate from her hand. It was clear we had moved up a little, into a neighborhood where people mowed their lawns. I never loved being outside as much as I did on Florence Street. We could breathe easier, sleep without swords.

Much of my world revolved around Noi's ways and rituals, which included eating fruit every night after dinner. Only now do I think of the journey each piece made, from orchards and trees to stores and bins and farmers' market baskets, to Noi's hands and shopping cart, to the kitchen sink for washing and rewashing, to the wrought-iron plate that lay untouched beneath the Buddha, back through Noi's hands into mine. In the evening, Noi unknotted the bun of her silver hair and let it pool around her like a cape. The apples and pears that Anh and I kept all day, waiting for just the right moment to eat, would be coaxed from us and whittled into symmetrical slices. The presentation meant a winding down into bedtime and made me feel warm, safe. Even then I loved order and disorder simultaneously, discretely. I loved to make detailed schedules planning every minute of my day (*2:00–2:30, Draw; 2:30–3:00, Get Anh to play Chinese checkers with me*), even while I kept my bed covered in a shock of books and dirty clothes.

Crissy usually made faces at Noi's fruit. She laughed at the way we sat cross-legged on the floor. I became self-conscious about our ritual, aware that it wasn't something Crissy was used to—aware that it might not be normal. We were in Rosa's house now, so the plate of orange wedges had to involve her, too. The moments Anh and I had always known with Noi—hoarding pieces of fruit while sharing the same green armchair to watch an episode of *Police Woman*—couldn't happen on Florence Street, where Rosa switched off the television when the noise of it got on her nerves.

One evening Rosa got to the fruit first. She liked mealy Red Delicious apples, the kind Noi never chose. Rosa cut them up carelessly, not bothering to peel the skin or make each piece the same size. "Eat," she said, setting the plate on the dining table. "An apple a day keeps the doctor away."

3

Dairy Cone

IN SAIGON WE LIVED IN THREE SMALL ROOMS SET IN A maze of concrete blocks. Here Noi raised four sons who, one by one, left to serve their mandatory years in the armed forces. Cuong, who repaired ships at the naval headquarters, and Anh at the nearby army communications base had lucky assignments. My father was lucky, too, having a friend who got him a position as a tank gunner. Quan was the one who became a ground soldier, sent to the countryside south of Saigon. He was killed two years later. The news devastated Noi. In the space of a few days her beautiful black hair, long enough to reach her knees, faded gray. One night, months after they buried his ashes, she had a dream that Quan was calling out for help. The next day she insisted that the family go to the cemetery, and when they got there they found that his headstone had fallen.

My grandmother was born in 1920, just outside Hanoi. As a girl she attended a French academy and had her teeth dyed lacquer-black, a traditional rite of beauty. When she married at twenty her husband had a burgeoning import business, selling everything from potatoes to jewelry to cigarettes. These were the good years, when Noi wore shimmering gold bracelets up and down her arms. She had a nanny for each child, silks for her *ao dai*s. But as the country sped toward partition, the North Vietnamese government targeted the educators, writers, business-people. My grandfather's contacts fell away; his company failed. Slowly they sold off their silks and jade. My grandmother's brace-lets, hidden carefully under long-sleeved blouses, became gold bartered for groceries.

One day my grandfather was taken away: interrogated, held in jail for weeks, stripped and beaten, ordered to reveal the anti-Communist ties he didn't have. My grandmother never speaks of this, his absence, the tension of each unknowing day. But my uncles say that when he was released he was a changed person. Not just broken, but brokenhearted. Just before the partition of Vietnam in 1954 the family fled south. It meant Noi leaving be-hind her four brothers and sisters, and it would be forty years before she would see them again.

Saigon meant freedom, a way to start over. They moved into one of the small cinderblock neighborhoods crowding the city and opened a store in the front room, selling odds and ends—stationery, games, candy. But my grandfather grew melancholy and depressed; he couldn't bring himself to begin anew. The store floundered, and each morning he woke up later and later. One fall day in 1959 my grandmother took a break from the empty store and went back to check on him. He had died, folded up in their bed. She said it was a heart attack or some kind of ill-ness. My uncle Chu Cuong said it was sadness. He was nine years old then, my father eleven.

Noi began selling *pho* and noodle dishes on the street corner

in the early mornings and evenings. She spent longer hours med-
itating and visiting the neighborhood temple. Her sons grew up,
and in between school classes learned to make money by gambling. My father prowled the billiards halls; Chu Cuong mas-
tered foosball. Years later, in a bar in the United States, a man
asked him to be his teammate in some national foosball champi-
onship game. Chu Cuong declined, but appreciated the American lesson: if you can make money on a game like that, he said,
you can make money on anything.

What happened between my grandfather's death and my
family's flight from Vietnam: too much, is what my father says,
and with never enough money. He, my uncles, and Grandmother
dispute each other's memories. Instead of talking about the war
they fixate on domestic details: Noi's pet chicken that went crazy
with rage at the color red; the neighborhood cricket fights and
how to catch a winning cricket; the family cat that brought them
birds for dinner and kept as a companion a little white rat.

Toward the end of the war, my father broke his arm during
an explosion—a minor injury that he stretched out for at least a
year—and an army friend supplied him with ample leave passes.
Hanging out in Saigon one hazy monsoon day, he met my mother.
She was sitting in a restaurant, and he walked over and said hello.
Later he took her to the movies; they sat in parks and traded
stories about their families. He brought her home to meet Noi.
They went out dancing. They fought and made up and fought
again. She stayed with her family and he stayed with his. They
went on together long enough to have my sister, then me. The
city was beginning to crumble, its future grim and foreseeable by
the end of August 1974. My father brought my sister and me to
Noi. Eight months later we'd be gone.

Before Florence Street, before Rosa, my father shopped for American groceries while Noi minded my sister and me at the Purple Cow ice cream parlor in Meijer Thrifty Acres. That's when I fell in love with ice cream. I was awed by the store: its enormity, the towering shelves, everything brightly boxed and labeled. It was its own city of happiness, a free-for-all, and nothing symbolized joy more than the Purple Cow herself, presiding over the ice cream counter. She was cardboard and wide, life-sized, her eyes drowsy, mouth in mid-moo.

The Vietnamese word for ice cream is *ca lem* and it's what I hear in my mind whenever I think of ice cream, the syllables colluding with the pleasure of that first lick of sweet cold. Probably this is because I spoke the word so often, begging Noi for more *ca lem, ca lem.* My favorites were chocolate or Superman—a neon tie-dye of fruit flavors—stuffed into nutty-brown sugar cones that dripped ice cream onto my clothes.

Meijer and the Saigon Market, both on 28th Street, became the epicenters of our lives, splitting our existence between two cultures. The Saigon Market meant home, familiar faces and foods, our own language, a general store for all things Vietnamese. Here my father plotted parties with his new friends while my grandmother and her friends gathered donations to start a Buddhist temple. It's strange to think how young my father was then, barely thirty years old.

Those early days seem a profusion of moments without structure. They return to me in vivid collage: the fizz of 7UP pouring out of a green bottle; the smell of the wild roses in the backyard; the day I watched a work crew install a stop sign at the end of the street. Probably we would have gone on like this for a long time, oblivious and drifting, without Rosa to tell us hard facts: words like *school, dentist,* and *English*—realms we needed to enter.

When Rosa bought ice cream she went for the giant plastic buckets that Noi could reuse as water pails and planters. She favored butter pecan, chocolate swirl, and mint chocolate chip. In our new household, ice cream had clear purposes: to appease, to distract, to mark happiness. Anh, Crissy, and I all had bowls of ice cream when Rosa came home from the hospital in March 1979 with our new brother, Vinh.

I do not recall Rosa or my father ever speaking of the pregnancy, no doubt because she had become pregnant before she and my father got married. Since that was associated with sex, and out-of-wedlock sex at that, it fell into the category of the unmentionable. I only learned of Vinh's imminent arrival when Crissy pointed to a squalling newborn on a TV show and said, "Mom's having a baby, too." I was four and a half years old when I held him for the first time, sitting on the edge of my parents' bed with Crissy and Anh, the idea of *brother* still incomprehensible. Vinh had had plenty of hair, black as mine, yet I felt no connection to him. Everything had happened too fast.

The fact of a son in the house pleased not only my father but Rosa a great deal, something I wouldn't understand until much later. She was still in the early stages of enthusiasm then, eager to solidify us into a family. She wanted my father's friends to be her friends, his community to be hers. When he took her to parties she stayed in the kitchen with the other wives, trying to learn

Vietnamese and get in on their conversations. She spoke the language the way white people sometimes spoke to us: too loud, enunciating each word slowly. Rosa's communications with Noi were comical. Trying to help Noi cook, she would hold up a bag of sugar and ask, "How much?" The words emerged as a shout, causing Noi to giggle uncontrollably.

Crissy made a point to learn as little Vietnamese as possible. She resented how her life had been changed around, and she hated sharing anything, especially a bedroom. She often referred to us as "Viennese" or "Vietmanese." Nonetheless, Anh and I looked up to Crissy. She had dark silky hair with natural waves, and to us everything she did, wore, and said was the coolest. Whatever she liked, we liked: Madonna, puffy lettering, Dr. Scholl's. When she wanted a dog we wanted one, too, and rejoiced when my father and Rosa relented. Crissy picked her out from the pound: a dirty-white Lhasa apso mix she named Mimi.

To celebrate Vinh's birth my father and Rosa threw a big party. Noi spent days in the kitchen, preparing piles of *cha gio* that she cooked in an electric fryer set up in the garage; shrimp cakes; platters heaped with *goi cuon*, fresh shrimp and vegetable spring rolls; *banh xeo*, delicate pancakes stuffed with meats, herbs, and bean sprouts; beef satay marinated in fish sauce, sugar, and lemongrass; mounds of vermicelli and rice for stewed shrimp; saucers filled with chilies swimming in *nuoc mam*. There were pasty dough balls stuffed with spiced pork and Chinese sausage; shrimp chips dyed in pastel colors, salty styrofoam that vanished on the tongue; pickled radishes, carrots, and cauliflower; heaps of dried coconut curls; dried persimmons, flat brown, each resembling a giant eye;

nubs of sugared pineapple and papaya; green bean cakes; red bean cakes. And always, the teardrop crunchy-tart pickled shallots that came in small cans labeled "pickled leeks." I would eat them even after my tongue burned from the brine. Noi never minded when I sneaked into the kitchen to grab the first shrimp chips, fresh from the deep fryer, a few *cha gio* cooling in a towel-lined colander, and extra pieces of the rich, salty-sweet Chinese sausage, blood red and shot through with white speckles of fat.

Anh and I were waitresses for the party, roles we would have for as long as parties lasted in that household. We fetched drinks and napkins while my father's friends beckoned to us, snapping their fingers. We were not the indulged little girls on Baldwin Street anymore, holding out our arms for a new toy or stick of gum. Now we were old enough to be useful, to wash dishes and do what we were told. Someone might want an extra beer or bean cake; another might need a dirty plate whisked away. Our heads were patted, cheeks pinched, shoulders grabbed while my father's friends assessed us out loud as good, thin, delicate, or clumsy.

The long hair we'd had on Baldwin Street had been clipped into the same bowl-shaped haircuts, later amended to Dorothy Hamill style, and for the party we wore identical patchwork dresses trimmed with rickrack. Anh and I liked to pretend we were twins. We had the same habit of finding hilarity at random moments—a stumble on the sidewalk, a glimpse of gaping-mouthed tennis shoes. But our similarities seemed to end there. She was lively and I was shy. She charmed everyone with her quick smile and perfect vision, while I had to wear horn-rimmed glasses too big for my face. Rosa had been the one to notice my poor eyesight, and these first glasses she'd chosen would set the precedent for the rest of my childhood—bulky plastic frames from the sale rack at the eye doctor's. I looked like a sorry version of my sister, and Rosa introduced us to the guests as "the pretty one and the smart one."

In the living room, people passed baby Vinh around as if he were an objet d'art, and in a way he was—multiracial, a child for the next century. When they finished admiring him they praised Anh and Crissy's pretty faces. I didn't mind slipping into the background. I was perpetually worried about breaking my glasses or being teased. I had discovered that adults liked to ask children questions only to laugh at their answers, and I hated being the butt of a joke, having to stand there and take it as a proper child should. *You're too shy, how are you going to get a husband?* someone might ask, setting the room into laughter.

Stealing a bowl of pickled leeks off the dining table, I slunk off to my top-bunk bed. I hid there with a book, eating the sour shallots until my eyes teared up, thinking of the block of Breyers Neapolitan ice cream that Chu Cuong had left waiting in the freezer. He sneered at buckets of ice cream, preferring, he said, the balance of sugar and cream in Breyers All Natural.

I didn't know it then, but Vinh's birth would signal the return of Rosa to her own family. She had grown up in a strict Catholic household, one of ten children—eight girls and two boys. Her parents were migrant workers who had come from Texas to follow the crop seasons in Michigan: sugar beets, cherries, blueberries, apples. They had settled in Fruitport, a small town near Lake Michigan. Most of Rosa's siblings thought she was hoity-toity, going off to Grand Valley State instead of getting married. But apart from one college semester in Denmark—a place she would talk about for years as though she had just come back—she hadn't gotten much farther than western Michigan. In Grand Rapids, working as a teacher after college, she got pregnant by a white guy who had no interest in marriage and children. So, alone, Rosa raised Crissy. Stung by her family's criticism, she became an atheist, immersed herself into left-wing activism—as much as was possible in Grand Rapids—and made her own life and career.

She was a strong woman, and we knew it in every word she spoke to us. But while her politics were liberal, when it came to what she called *personal matters* she was silent. On this she and my father never disagreed. Subjects such as Crissy's father, my and Anh's mother, and sex, especially sex, fell into the category of the taboo. Danger! Warning! Look away! We could watch cop shows and kung fu movies all day, but if a scene or a song referenced sex, then the whole production risked being shut down. We were even supposed to change the channel when people kissed on TV, as if seeing such an act would shift us into becoming *bad girls*.

When *Flashdance* came out (which we weren't allowed to see) my sisters and I fell in love with Irene Cara's "What a Feelin'." The lyrics seemed innocuous enough. *Take your passion and make it happen!* But I misheard the words and one day Rosa caught me singing, *Take your pants off, and make it happen!* She rushed over to the radio and snapped it off, saying that song was banned from then on. When I asked why, she said, "None of your business."

For the most part, though, she and my father weren't consistent in enforcing their rules. It kept us kids off-kilter, a little paranoid, which was maybe their goal. Rosa herself loved to sing along to Rita Coolidge, proclaiming *your love is lifting me higher*, though the lyrics veered toward the obscene with *quench my desire*.

And she couldn't resist the lilting tempo of the Pointer Sisters' *I want a man with a slow hand*. It was years before I understood what the song meant.

On our own, out of earshot, my sisters and I had learned all the words to Olivia Newton-John's "Physical" and Air Supply's "Making Love out of Nothing at All." Anh and Crissy would play Chu Cuong's Eagles records and sing right along to "Hotel California." We learned what to watch and listen to in private, under cover, whenever our parents weren't around. Such silence and secrecy became a natural part of our family, circling our household like an electric fence.

If their equal sense of strength and will had brought my father and Rosa together, it also became a source of complication. They were two people struggling against the wall of the conservative norm that defined Grand Rapids, and sometimes they turned on each other. My father might appreciate Rosa's posted list of household chores, divided up by person and day, but that same list could also send him into inexplicable fury. Rosa wanted to fit in with my father's crowd, but resented their drunken parties.

One of Rosa's rules was that we had to ask permission for snacks. We could not, for instance, grab a wafer cookie without first clearing it with her. We couldn't ask Noi because she would say yes to any food we wanted and would bring us fruit twice a day anyway. Nor could we ask our father, who had been used to indulging us with candy and chips. "But Dad said I could" didn't fly with her. Invoking the price of groceries, she would deny my requests about half the time, depending on whether or not she believed I was truly hungry, or if I had finished my last meal. She continually invoked *taxes* and *bills*, words that echoed throughout my childhood.

So I began stealing food.

I would bring a book with me, pretending to be on my way to the basement to do some reading. If Rosa was in the living room she couldn't see the kitchen but could hear everything, so I had to move silently. More often than not she would be working at the dining table, in full view of the kitchen. I would wait for her to go to the bathroom or become otherwise distracted, then hoist myself up onto the counter, open the cupboard, reach for the cookies—I knew exactly where they were, of course—and take away a handful, hiding them behind my book. All done in a matter of seconds. In the summer, I tucked popsicles into the waistband of my shorts, shielding the evidence with another book. I honed my method over the years so that I could slide in and out of the kitchen with nearly entire meals carried between my shorts and T-shirt. I brought my spoils up to my bunk bed, where they could be hidden under the sheets if necessary. If Crissy and Anh were there and in a tattletale mood I would retreat to Noi's closet. I sat there often, peaceful among her *ao dai*s, hand-knitted sweaters, and sensible shoes, reading, writing notes to myself, and eating my contraband.

Ice cream was the one thing nearly impossible to steal, though I could swipe spoonfuls at a time, but luckily my uncles swooped in to provide. They gave Anh and me plenty of change so we could chase down the ice cream trucks that crawled through the neighborhood. Even from far away I could discern their carousel tunes, and perked up like a dog detecting its master's whistle. Depending on my mood I would choose a Drumstick, coated in chocolate and nuts, or a red, white, and blue Bomb Pop that had a gumball suspended at its tip. Anh usually selected an orange Push-Up or a Creamsicle. We would ride away on our bicycles, steering with one hand and eating ice cream with the other, feeling victorious. Crissy was usually too busy with her friends to bother with the ice cream truck, but she never missed out on the Dairy Cone, our beacon on 28th Street between the Witmark Merchandise Store and the Saigon Market.

The Dairy Cone had a plastic sky-blue awning and walls covered in faded photographs of delectable desserts that instantly replaced the love I had nursed for the Purple Cow. The words *parfait, turtle sundae, upside-down banana split* made my heart thrill. On the rare times that Rosa took us to the Dairy Cone she only let us order the standard soft-serves—chocolate, vanilla, or twist, thirty-nine cents each. Duly the blond teenage girl behind the counter would hold the plain cone to the machine and pull the lever, extracting a steady flow of ice cream in rhythmic swirls. I had no complaints about the soft-serve, but the bigger items on the menu beckoned. All along the counter sat buckets of cherries and sprinkles, and vats of chocolate, caramel, and strawberry sauce.

Chu Cuong and Chu Dai took us to the Dairy Cone once or twice a week all summer long, and urged us to order anything we wanted. Crissy and Anh favored banana splits, mainly for the sheer excess and the fuchsia-colored maraschino cherries. I alternated between sundaes and parfaits, contemplating the different interplays of ice cream, hot fudge, and nuts. I especially loved the airy whiteness of whipped cream billowing out of a can, a sophisticated leap from the Cool Whip we had with pumpkin pie on holidays. Sitting at the Dairy Cone's picnic table under the fluo-

rescence of 28th Street, I would carve out each mouthful of *ca lem*
with a pink plastic spoon. I could never eat fast enough to avoid
the puddles of melted cream at the bottom of the dish. But my
uncles didn't mind or call me greedy. They didn't worry about
things like that. They ate what they liked and however much
suited them, and no one could tell them otherwise. In the basement they had set up leather recliners and a stereo system and
they had all kinds of records and tapes, from Van Morrison and
the Rolling Stones to Lionel Richie and ABBA. (I especially admired how regally the ABBA ladies stood in their slinky white
clothes, spotlit, defying the dark crowding close on the *Super
Trouper* album.) Chu Cuong and Chu Dai bought what they desired, dined when they chose, and came and left at any hour.
Theirs was a freewheeling, independent life, or so it seemed, and
I couldn't wait to be grown up so I could be like them, eating
whatever I wanted and doing whatever I wanted, without permission.

4

Fast Food Asian

THE VIETNAMESE COMMUNITY IN GRAND RAPIDS CAME together around the Saigon Market on 28th Street. Sandwiched between an auto body shop and the Waterbed Gallery, the store's tiny space was crammed with dried fish, fruit, canisters of tea, and giant sacks of rice that doubled as beanbags. The air, redolent with something musty and musky—old sandalwood layered with mung bean noodles—seeped into our hair and clothes. To keep us occupied my father would buy my sister and me sweet-and-sour plums, Botan rice candy, and bags of dried squid, telling us to go look at waterbeds and cars. Anh and I wanted waterbeds very badly. We imagined floating rather than sleeping, rafts permanently moored. We never had enough nerve to go into the store and jump on the beds, make waves. So we stood in the parking lot, where broken glass made a trail to the overflowing dumpsters in the back, and shared the dried squid, untangling the long ochre-colored strands and curling them into our mouths. Later, at home, the squid's pungent odor on our hands would send Crissy running away, screaming, "NASTY!"

Inside the Saigon Market, my father and his friends hung out at the checkout counter, surrounded by displays of jade and gold jewelry and mini Buddhas. They could spend hours laughing and talking to the owner, Thanh, who laughed loudest of all. Thanh gave away free scroll calendars to every customer, and he had a big new house in a cul-de-sac subdivision in Kentwood. The more money he made, the more family members he was able to sponsor. They trickled in monthly and soon he bought the house across the street for his in-laws. Thanh wanted to be the don of the community. Balding, shaped like a white man, he wore Hawaiian print shirts and flip-flops year-round. His protruding belly was the physical symbol of his success. He was the first to throw Saturday night parties that went on forever, where the men played Vietnamese poker for increasingly high stakes, worked their way through bottles of Courvoisier and Hennessy VSOP, and told raucous, bawdy stories about their boyhoods in Vietnam. The women were relegated to the kitchen to gossip and compare information like which brand of makeup to buy (Lancôme was the favorite). Noi always took over the cooking. Like the other grandmothers, she supervised the kitchen and served as principal to us kids. Three or more generations in one household—that was the Vietnamese way. It meant built-in child care and cooking, and a consistent, tidy home. Noi was the person I saw when I woke up, when I came home from school, and before I went to bed.

The combination of Vietnam's ancient matrilineal roots, Confucianism, and Western influences made for a modern-day balance of control and deference in every household. As the oldest in our family, Noi was the nominal head. She sat at the head of the table, always got the first serving at dinner, and rode in the front seat of the car. At the same time, she was in charge of raising the children and taking care of the home. My father was supposed to be the breadwinner, the disciplinarian. He need ask no one for guidance, tell no one his plans; whatever he said or did had to be accommodated by the rest of the family. Rosa, the wife and mother, hovered somewhere in between. In other households I saw that the role could be nervous, anxious with watching, jumping in, smoothing things over. Or it could be contentious, filled with clashes with husband and mother-in-law—that age-old battle for domestic sovereignty. The mothers worked, too, all of them seamstresses or detail workers at factories. While the women had social lives mostly bound by family, the men had poker games nearly every Saturday night. Rosa, who had campaigned for the Equal Rights Amendment, could only take so much of this arrangement. She was the breadwinner, too, and she had every intention of running the household. She was astonished by my father's claim to freedom, and their fights about how he spent money or time escalated into middle-of-the-night shouts. I don't remember what they said, what words they flung, but none of it stopped the poker games or drinking parties.

My stepmother stood apart from the women in the kitchen. She didn't know how to speak Vietnamese or cook Vietnamese food. She didn't wear *ao dai*s or jade bracelets. Her expansive chest and curly hair made the thin, straight-haired women seem even thinner. They smiled at her, spoke a little English—*How are you?*—then went back to their own conversations. Rosa spent these parties washing dishes, cleaning up, trying to be useful. She often sat alone in the living room, holding Vinh while he slept.

Anh and I hung out with the other kids in the basement, playing Atari and ping-pong and watching TV. The commercials held our interest as much as any show, for they let us know what we should be eating, playing, and wearing. They let us know how we should be. After a commercial for Lite-Brite a girl with shiny pink barrettes might triumph, "*My* ma and ba me bought that." Another kid would boast about going to McDonald's three times in one week.

Almost all these kids were way ahead of me and Anh. Their parents were anxious for them to fit into Grand Rapids and found the three quickest avenues: food, money, and names. Food meant American burgers and fries. Money meant Jordache jeans and Izod shirts. Names meant a whole new self. Overnight, Thanh's children, Truoc and Doan, became Tiffany and David, and other families followed. Huong to Heather, Quoc to Kevin, Lien to Lynette. Most of the kids chose their own names and I listened while they debated the merits of Jennifer versus Michelle, Stephanie versus Crystal. They created two lives for themselves: the American one and the Vietnamese one—*Oriental,* as we all said back then. Out in the world they were Tiffany and David; at home they were Truoc and Doan. The mothers cooked two meals—*pho* and sautés for the elders, Campbell's soup and Chef Boyardee for the kids.

Rosa would have none of it. She hadn't changed her own name when she married, after all, and had named my brother Vinh—not some white name, she scoffed. She told Anh and me that we needed to be proud of who we were. Still, my sister tried out Ann for a little while, until laziness prevailed and she went back to Anh. It was an easy name anyway, and caused her little stress. Not like my name: Bich. In Vietnamese it meant jade, which was all well and fine in Vietnam but meant nothing in Michigan. It was pronounced with an accent tilting up, the tone leading almost toward a question, with a silent h. *Bic!* I hated the sound—too harsh, too hard, and the *c* so slight that it evaporated in the air. I preferred to hear it as *Bit*. The sound seemed tidier, quieter. So that's what I made my name over to be, and it was fine until my classmates learned to read and swear. By second grade I was being regularly informed that I was a bitch. I started fantasizing then about being Beth, or maybe Vanessa or Polly. I longed to be Jenny Adams with the perfect simple name to match her perfect honeyed curls. But I knew I could never make it stick. Who would listen to me? Who would allow me to change? Not Rosa, nor anyone at school. I could not tell my stepmother, my father, my sister—I could tell no one—what I suffered each day during roll call. The shame layered upon embarrassment equaled silence. I felt I could judge the nature and compassion of teachers, especially substitutes, by the way they read my name. The good ones hesitated and gently spelled it, avoiding a phonetic pronunciation. The evil ones simply called out, *Bitch? Bitch Nu-guy-in?*

So I listened carefully, enviously, while the kids in Thanh's basement transformed themselves into true Americans. Most of their parents had factory jobs, too, but that didn't stop them from buying nice clothes and tennis shoes and toys, whatever it took to assimilate. Rosa wouldn't have that, either. She believed in *pinching pennies,* as she put it, and my longing for a Jenny Adams wardrobe was useless against her rules about clothes. Rosa favored reds and burgundies, claiming they were best for our skin types, and she forbade me and Anh from wearing yellow. "Never, never, never," she said. "Girls with your skin color look sallow in yellow." When we shopped we hit the discount stores. Her favorite was Burlington Coat Factory, which in spite of its name mostly sold clothes. They were piled in giant bins or stuffed tight into circular hanging displays. On principle alone Rosa purchased only what was on sale, her eyes lighting up at the word *clearance*. When I went to school in blue corduroys and a pink sweater stitched with a picture of a stallion rearing up, I avoided sitting next to Jenny Adams with her flowered dresses and polished Mary Janes.

While the other girls in Thanh's basement learned to dress like Jenny, I found comfort in the girl whose parents were as stubborn as mine: Loan, who remained Loan, which carried a lovely double syllabic. *Lo-an.* We went to the same school during first and second grade, and became the best of friends. Bitch and Loan, some of the kids said on the playground. *Hey, bitch, can you loan me some money?*

At home, I kept opening the refrigerator and cupboards, wishing for American foods to magically appear. I wanted what the other kids had: Bundt cakes and casseroles, Chee•tos and Doritos. My secret dream was to bite off just the tip of every slice of pizza in the two-for-one deal we got at Little Caesar's. The more American foods I ate, the more my desires multiplied, outpacing any interest in Vietnamese food. I had memorized the menu at Dairy Cone, the sugary options in the cereal aisle at Meijer's, and every inch of the candy display at Gas City: the rows of gum, the rows with chocolate, the rows without chocolate. I knew the spartan packs of Juicy Fruit as well as the fat pillows of Bubble Yum, Bubbalicious, Hubba Bubba, Chewels,

Tidal Wave, the shreds of Big League Chew, and the gum shaped into hot dogs and hamburgers. I knew Reese's peanut butter cups, Twix, Heath Crunch, Nestlé Crunch, Baby Ruth, Bar None, Oh Henry!, Mounds and Almond Joy, Snickers, Mr. Goodbar, Watchamacallit, Kit Kat, Chunky, Charleston Chew, Alpine White, Ice Cubes, Whoppers, PayDay, Bonkers, Sugar Babies, Milk Duds, Junior Mints. Bottle caps, candy cigarettes, candy necklaces, and wax lips. Starburst, Skittles, Sprees, Pixy Stix, Pop Rocks, Ring Pops, SweeTarts, Lemonheads, Laffy Taffy, Fun Dip, Lik-m-Aid, Now and Later, Gobstoppers, gummy worms, Nerds, and Jolly Ranchers. I dreamed of taking it all, plus the freezer full of popsicles and nutty, chocolate-coated ice cream drumsticks. I dreamed of Little Debbie, Dolly Madison, Swiss Miss, all the bakeries presided over by prim and proper girls.

When Rosa cooked on some weekend nights she kept to a repertoire of sloppy joes made with ketchup, tacos with ground beef flavored with spices from the cupboard, meat loaf tinged with cumin, Mexican rice, goulash, pot roast cooked in a pressure cooker until the meat was soft and stringy, and her specialty dish of *sopa*—ground beef, stewed tomatoes, and egg noodles cooked in a skillet until the noodles burned. These were sensible, no-waste foods. But she wasn't immune to convenience, sometimes buying boxes of instant mashed potatoes or scalloped potatoes, whose hard slices looked just like plastic before they got baked in seasoning mix and milk. Rosa would also consent to a few cans of Beefaroni, frozen Banquet pot pies, and boxes of brandless macaroni and cheese. I was always begging her to buy the boxed lasagna kit from Chef Boyardee. I loved to assemble the lasagna, careful to spread the sauce and cheese so each layer contained equal allocations. If no one was looking I would eat a cold half spoonful of the sweet, beef-tinted sauce. I loved to sniff the grated cheese and let a pinch of it dissolve on my tongue. It was a sharper, smellier smell than the Colby and generic singles Rosa occasionally bought; usually, though, we just wore down the brick of government cheese she got a few times a year from the surplus pile at the Hispanic Institute. She drew the line at Hamburger Helper. Despite my private opinion, she believed she didn't need such a helper and certainly not at those prices.

As with clothes shopping, sales trumped all. I believed she would have fed us Cracker Jacks and Ding Dongs every day if they had been on permanent markdown. She also had clear preferences, like olive loaf instead of bologna, orange Faygo instead of Crush, raisin cookies instead of chocolate chip. She sprinkled wheat germ on grapefruit and bought maple sugar oatmeal over peaches and cream. These small differences accumulated within my growing stockpile of shame and resentment, as if Rosa herself were preventing me from fitting in and being like everyone else. I wrinkled my face at her *sopa* and the mound of rice she served with shards of dry chicken. I scowled at almost everything we ate, even Noi's *pho*, shrimp stews, and curries. I wanted to savor new food, different food, white food. I was convinced I was falling far behind on becoming American, and then what would happen to me? I would be an outcast the rest of my days.

But Rosa did not want to be like the Vander Wals next door. She called their midwestern dinners bland, sticking out her tongue for emphasis. She might cook a pot roast, but it was different—

richer, she insisted, with *real* flavor. White American food was as repugnant to her as tulips and the Dutchness and conservatism they represented. Not that I understood this then. I didn't know that Rosa might have felt oppressed in this cold climate, suffocated and isolated. I hadn't arrived at that point yet. I was still in the stage of longing: all I wanted was to sit at the dinner table and eat pork chops the way my friends did. Because I could not, because our household did not, I invested such foods with power and allure.

Rosa had put an end to my father's bringing home candy and gum and Pringles, but when he got a craving he pursued it. He loved Jell-O parfait from the deli aisle, sweet gherkins, braunschweiger, Chicken in a Biskit, two-liter bottles of pop, and cream-filled wafer cookies dyed pink and orange. (I tried to pit him against Rosa's shopping, encouraging him to consider French onion dip to accompany the bargain bag of Jays, or better yet Tato Skins for their "baked potato appeal," as the commercials promised.) He was fond of gadgets and purchased the first microwave oven on our street. I bragged about it to all of my friends. The microwave was so American in its efficiency and sleekness, with its green digital display and buttons that beeped whenever I touched them. In a flash I could make my favorite snack of instant cocoa and baked potatoes.

One thing the whole family could agree on was fast food. Like the Chicken Coop, which offered up tubs of fried chicken with delicate, super-crispy coatings that smelled of butter, herbs, and fat. Happy were the evenings my father brought home an extra-large bucket, with sides of coleslaw, biscuits and honey, and mashed potatoes and gravy. Anh and I liked the drumsticks for their portability and ease, and because kids on Shake 'n Bake commercials always looked so happy crunching on them. Crissy only ate the white meat of the breast. My father, uncles, Noi, and Rosa reached for the thighs where the meat was darkest and juiciest. When at last only bones remained, cleaned by my father and Noi, Anh and I picked up the little fried bits left at the bottom of the bucket. We tipped it back into our wide-open mouths to catch every last crumb.

The Chicken Coop napkins were printed with laughing roosters and somber psalms. *Upon the wicked He shall rain snares, fire and brimstone, and a horrible tempest: this shall be the portion of their cup.* The words turned translucent from the grease on our hands. When I asked Rosa what such sayings meant she snapped, "They mean nothing," and threw the napkins away.

In the fall of 1982 Burger King launched a campaign to make the Whopper America's number one hamburger. My father happened to love the char-grilled taste of Whoppers—the tomato and onion, creamy with mayonnaise and ketchup; the thin slices of pickle. Burger King was a family treat, and any car ride toward it meant blissful calmness; no one dared to fight and ruin the experience. One day my father heard that Burger King was running a fantastic promotion: to celebrate winning a national taste test they were giving away free Whoppers for one day only. All you had to do was step up to the counter, say, "Whopper beat the Big Mac," and you'd get a free Whopper Junior, one per person. To the Burger King my family urgently repaired, wondering if we would get there in time, and if the place would run out of burgers. There was quite a line at the restaurant, which created an audience for each person's statement. My father spoke the words proudly, having rehearsed them in the car. Rosa went next, then Crissy and Anh, then me. I froze. Suddenly it felt like everyone was staring at me, and I lost the ability to speak. For one terrible minute I was the stupid, funny-looking girl to mock and deride.

My father nudged me, then made a *tsk*-ing clicking sound. It was the noise he made when he was getting angry. I knew how swiftly that noise could escalate into a shout, his red-faced temper taking over. He would hurl keys, plates, shoes—anything nearby—against a wall. Out of the corner of my eye I could see my sisters looking intently away, as if already separating themselves from me, freeing themselves from tangential blame. I leaned forward and whispered, "Whopper beat the Big Mac."

My father clapped, and I got my burger. He ordered fries and pop for everyone, and as we claimed a table I saw how happy he was. He was practically cackling, as though being here with our free Whoppers signified some true victory.

Noi was the holdout. She might go along with us to Burger King, and would even accept a few fries, but her disdain for the place was as visible as the paper crowns Anh and I wore while we ate. Noi had little use for American food. She would have preferred to avoid it completely, but she couldn't ignore the way I started pushing her beef and onion sautés around my plate. I hadn't stopped liking her food—*cha gio* and pickled vegetables still held an iron grip on my heart—but now I knew what real people ate. And in my mind I used that term: *real people*. Real people did not eat *cha gio*. Real people ate hamburgers and casseroles and brownies. And I wanted to be a real person, or at least make others believe that I was one.

The closest Noi came to cooking American food was making french fries her way, wedge-cut, served with vinegar and lettuce, and thin steaks pan-fried with onion and garlic. These, along with a bowl of my favorite *mi* soup—shrimp-flavor Kung-Fu ramen— made lunches and dinners to dream about. Still, I knew that no one at school had homemade french fries, or ramen. No one at school knew how I really ate. They didn't know how much time I spent thinking of dinner, of stolen popsicles, of ways for a Whopper to rise up and beat, once and for all, the Big Mac.

For I realized that the other kids scorned Burger King. McDonald's was the cool thing, and at recess girls clapped hands with each other and sang, *Hamburger, filet-o-fish, cheeseburger, french fries, icy Coke, thick shakes, sundaes, and apple pies.* They even had birthday parties in the McDonald's playroom, where each girl got her own Happy Meal with a Strawberry Shortcake figurine. The Whopper had a long way to go to beat the Big Mac. In the gaze of my classmates I understood the satisfaction of symmetrical yellow arches. Even the hamburgers were tidier, more self-contained; no one at McDonald's spilled onion and ketchup with each bite. The very word *McDonald's* rolled more easily off the tongue—a sturdy lilting name, nothing there to make fun of, against the guttural, back-of-the-throat emphasis of *Burger*. Once in a while Chu Cuong and Chu Dai alleviated my fast food sorrow by taking my siblings and me to McDonald's. Despite my father and Burger King's campaign, Chu Cuong had developed a fondness for the Big Mac, and he always ordered dessert: apple or cherry pies, deep-fried, gorgeously oblong and brown and burning hot as they slid out of their thin cardboard sleeves.

Chu Cuong and Chu Dai were also the ones who drank extravagant amounts of Sprite, shunning the two-liters of RC and Squirt we usually had in the house. They let us kids keep the cans for the deposits—ten cents in Michigan, which added up fast for candy purchases. Chu Cuong would toss his empty pop cans into the backseat of his blue Thunderbird and wait until they piled up, a shimmering mosaic of silver and green. Then after we collected them in trash bags he'd ferry us to Meijer's bottle return center. Carrying the sacks across the parking lot, he was like a vision of a Vietnamese Santa.

Next door, the Vander Wals' oldest daughter, Jennifer, was almost my age. She was blond with matching socks and unscuffed shoes. When summer emerged we found ourselves face to face across the strip of grass that separated our driveways, just bored enough with our siblings to become friends with each other.

Jennifer introduced me to the concept of homemade, which I only associated with American food, when she gave me half of a cookie her mother had baked. Nestlé's Toll House, she called it, and I thought, You name your cookies? But it was like no cookie I had ever had. It was crumbly and rich, the chocolate chips bearing no resemblance to the pinpoints found in Chips

Ahoy. In our house, cookies came from Keebler, Nabisco, or, more frequently, the generic company whose label shouted "COOKIES" in stark black letters. Once in a while, at my father's request, Rosa brought home Voortman windmill cookies, or the cream-filled pink and yellow wafers that were as dull to me as graham crackers.

The concept of homemade cookies struck me as suspect and impossible. "What do you mean, your mom made them?" I demanded.

Jennifer tried to explain the flour and sugar and Crisco, her mother's big mixing bowl and cookie sheets. I had thought all American food came from a package and some mystical factory process. The idea that a person could create such a thing at home was a revelation. And then, a desire.

I wondered how many more layers of discovery stood between me and true Americanness. I decided that even if Rosa wouldn't let me change my name, I could change myself anyway. I could keep secrets: from my white friends at school and from my family at home. At school I was good, as neat with my homework as any other girl and just as well behaved. At home I stole food, sulked in my grandmother's closet, and in fits of unexplained rage threw Rosa's clean clothes down the laundry chute.

It was exhausting, this secrecy, this effort to be normal, and I took to wandering the house at night when everyone else was asleep. I liked being invisibly in-between, a shadow dissolving into itself. My father and stepmother believed in silence and fear; they made strict rules to contain their possible unraveling. In truth, I had a thousand questions about my face and my race, but it was so much easier to deny them than to speak out loud and court the embarrassment and shame that always lay in wait for me. As I stood at the living room window, the street lamps seemed to cast an eerie glow over the neighborhood. I wrapped myself in the yellowed nylon curtains my stepmother had hung and wondered what it would be like to live in any other house.

5

Toll House Cookies

EVERY SUMMER MORNING JENNIFER VANDER WAL, MY next-door neighbor, friend, and enemy, would ring the doorbell and ask if I wanted to go play. I always did, and we would spend our daylight hours running from her house to mine, riding bicycles, and listening for the ice cream truck to roll through the neighborhood. Jennifer and I worked a trade-off. She had a basement of dreams, a trove of Legos, construction paper, and crayons— the full Crayola 64, not the pallid Kmart version my parents bought. I could offer video games, *Days of Our Lives,* and MTV. Barbie dolls, too, or at least the knockoff version, Cindy, whose shiny breasts Jennifer's parents had forbidden from their house.

Summer arrived when the ChemLawn truck pulled up in front of Jennifer's yard. Her father, Cal, was a music teacher and spent warm days fixating on his garden. He pruned and weeded in his pressed shorts, knee-high black socks, and Hush Puppies. *A Dutch gardener,* Rosa called him, rolling her eyes.

Jennifer's mother, Linda, was a soft-fleshed woman with a singsong voice. She gave occasional piano lessons but spent most of her time cleaning. Her kitchen was so clean it looked like no one ever cooked there. But Linda did cook, of course. She served lunch at noon and dinner at six o'clock, and in the afternoon she baked Toll House cookies, stashing them in a glossy blue jar. Linda's fears were all about stains—Kool-Aid, grass, chocolate milk. She fretted over dirt, lined the hallways with plastic runners. Sometimes, like a Cheer commercial come to life, she hung bright towels on a clothesline in the backyard.

Jennifer was one year younger than I, but she was taller, bigger, her manners mimicking an adult's. She had her father's deepset blue eyes and her mother's efficient, can-do demeanor. She had a habit of running her hands inside the waistband of her shorts, and she licked the space below her lower lip compulsively, so that a pink swath formed there. I liked this about her, this glimpse of lack of control. On Sundays she wore frilled dresses to church and had to stay indoors. Once, Vinh and I sat in the backyard with a box of Lemonheads and stuffed tufts of grass through the chain-link fence that divided our backyard from the Vander Wals'. There was something satisfying about seeing the grass fall on the other side. Part littering, part disappearing.

My father and Jennifer's father hated each other. The hatred was immediate and visceral, plain as the view up Sycamore Street to 36th, where Jennifer and I were not supposed to walk. It drove Cal crazy that his immaculate property had to sit next to ours. Every few days his lawn mower cut a clear boundary between their emerald grass and our lazy thatch. The Vander Wals' driveway was smooth, ending at a two-staller with a fiberglass automatic door. Our driveway was splotched with oil. When my stepmother's '71 Toyota—avocado-green, almost the exact shade of the vinyl siding on our house—died in the driveway, it stayed there for years. The garage was packed with boxes, tools, broken bicycles, all the junk my parents couldn't bring themselves to throw away.

Once in a while, after my father got home from his shift at North American Feather, he would drag out the old lawn mower that always took a dozen tries before it coughed to life. He would work shirtless, singing Vietnamese songs whose words I never learned.

When I think of Jennifer, I think of cloudless afternoons ripening toward sunset and dinner. As the hour approached I would always ask what her mother was making. She would go to the kitchen to find out. "Shake 'n Bake," she'd report. "Pot roast." "Macaroni Helper." Once I ducked under their dining room window to listen to the sounds of their dinnertime. They must have prayed before each meal, but I only remember the ting of forks against plates, the soft slur of a serving spoon carving out a heap of scalloped potatoes.

Jennifer was afraid of Noi's food. *Pho*, stewed beef and eggs, shrimp curry, noodle dishes with *nuoc mam* and coriander. "No, thank you," was her polite reply every time Noi offered her something to eat. Jennifer kept her hands behind her back as she shook her head.

One summer day she showed up in my backyard with two of her friends from vacation Bible school. I was playing on the swing set, which was the envy of the neighborhood. It was solid and sturdy like the ones on a playground, and if you were brave you could sail right out of your swing and try to land standing on the grass.

Jennifer and her friends matched, all pleated shorts and flower barrettes, all various heads of blond, and I dared them to swing as high as they could and jump off. They refused. "My mom will kill me if I get my clothes dirty," one of the girls said.

"I got mud on my Sunday clothes and got in big trouble," Jennifer put in.

"By the way, girls," said the one with pink socks folded down at the ankle, "Aren't you glad the Lord is always with us?"

Quick as my father's temper igniting, I said, "I don't believe in the Lord."

She dropped to her knees, eyes closed, and clasped her hands together. The other girl pointed to the sky, whispering, "She's praying to God for you."

A silence fell over us. At last the girl in the pink socks opened her eyes and stood.

"I'm going to pray for you every night," she promised.

Solemnly the other girl asked me, "Were you baptized?"

"No, she wasn't," Jennifer answered, and that's when I knew the whole scene had been orchestrated for my benefit. These girls hadn't come to my yard to play; they had come to save me.

I could see my grandmother checking on us through the window in the kitchen, where she must have been starting dinner. Maybe salty shrimp with scallions, my sister's favorite. I said the only thing I could say, because now it was a matter of pride: "There is no God."

The girl who had prayed for me covered her face. "You can't say that! You can't say that!" And she began to cry.

That summer Jennifer turned seven and her parents threw her a big birthday party. My sister and I showed up early and hung out in the backyard, where Cal Vander Wal's rock and flower garden sloped down the hill to a patio set up for party games. Pink and purple balloons bobbed from the lawn chairs and hung from the clothesline. I was excited for the ice cream and cake, and the party favors Jennifer had promised. Then Jennifer's friends, the ones from her real life—church and Clearbrook Christian School—appeared. They floated toward us, dressed in white like the birthday girl. A few months later, when I first heard that song from *The Sound of Music*—*girls in white dresses with blue satin sashes*—I recalled with bitter and astonished poignancy that moment on the hill. It seemed to replay itself, forever in slow motion, in my mind. Later, when my birthday rolled around, Jennifer brought me a little white box with a blue adhesive bow. When she put it in my hands I saw that it was nothing but a piece of paper folded into a cube. I opened it:

G

S O N

D

S

Every immigrant knows the dual life, marked by a language at home and a language outside. For me it was also the face I saw in the mirror. It was the smell of rice simmering in its cooker. The statue of Buddha in Noi's bedroom. None of these made sense when I played with Jennifer, but the second I came home they were mine all over again.

I remember being invited into Jennifer's kitchen—I was not allowed just to walk in, the way she did in our house—and gazing with wonder at the cleared countertops, the sink uncluttered with dishes, everything *clean as a whistle,* as Jennifer's mother might have said. I called her Mrs. Vander Wal; Jennifer called my stepmother Rosa. "She can't possibly be your *real* mom," Jennifer had said to me once. I refused to admit to her how much I didn't know.

Linda Vander Wal smiled her soft-cheeked smile. She had light, painted-on eyebrows, her one vanity. She opened the freezer door and removed a tray of homemade Kool-Aid popsicles, giving one to Jennifer, one to her brother Paul, and one to me. This event happened but two or three times a summer. Never mind that these popsicles didn't even taste that good—you could suck out all the juice, leaving a pale block of ice. I would hold the plastic popsicle holder and eat the frozen Kool-Aid as if it were the only delicacy I would ever have. From the kitchen I could see the living room piano and curvy-armed sofa. I'd hardly ever stepped foot in that room, the showpiece of the house, used only when "company" came over. It was for grown-ups, Jennifer said. Off the path of the plastic runners, it glimmered like a vision of candy in a fairy tale.

For years my father and Jennifer's father maintained their silent hatred—the curt hello, the briefest nod, the distance in their faces. My sister and I absorbed this feeling, too. "I'd like to beat him up," Anh would say about Cal, gritting her teeth. "I wish Dad would punch his lights out."

One late afternoon in the summer of 1983 Jennifer and I were playing hopscotch in her driveway while our younger brothers pulled each other around in a wagon. It was almost time for Linda to call out dinnertime, and I was filled with a quiet, tenebrous feeling that I would recognize years later as a sense of responsibility. I didn't know what it meant then, only that it hit me hardest when I came home in the evenings and Noi dished me up a bowl of *canh chua*, or beef and noodles. Falling asleep on one of the reject pillows from North American Feather, I would feel as though I'd forgotten something important.

Cal Vander Wal was working on the tulip beds in front of his house; my father was picking some Vietnamese herbs he had planted in our backyard. Those days, Rosa was either working or at night school, and I felt a sense of suspended time when I stepped inside our house. There were no bedtimes or bath times, no order to the evenings.

In Jennifer's driveway her brother Paul stood up in the wagon. Jennifer screamed even before he crashed onto the pavement. In an instant Cal was there, yelling at Vinh, and suddenly here was Linda and my father and Anh barreling into view. My father and Cal faced each other—my father shirtless, Cal standing tall in his starched short sleeves and knee-highs—and they were shouting. The sound of their voices blurred. *Who do you think you are? Shut up. You better tell him— You better watch it—*

And then my father lunged. He was much smaller than Cal, but he had spent his youth in Saigon, gambling and running away from the police. Cal, for all his time spent outdoors, was spindly and wan. But in the second that my father might have struck, fulfilling my sister's treasured wish, he stopped. It must have taken every restraint within him, and I realized then how much my sister's wish was my own, how much I'd wanted the crack of fist against face, Cal falling into his prized green lawn. I wanted something to be smashed and broken—the paradigm unspoken that ran between us like the chain-link fence in the backyard.

That was when the balance between friendship and enmity broke for good, and Jennifer and I began competing with possessions: puffy stickers, Trapper Keepers, neon socks. This would go on for years, following the waves of Cabbage Patch dolls, rubber bracelets, and paint-splattered clothing. I would brag about the Sheena Easton, Prince, and Madonna songs she wasn't allowed to listen to at home, and Jennifer would show off her well-stocked toy box and trays of colored pencils.

My heart ached when Jennifer's parents finished the rest of their basement and created a new room and next-door bathroom just for her. "Too bad," she said, "you'll always have to share a room with Anh."

The bedroom had fawn-colored carpeting and pink floral wallpaper, a white dresser with brass pulls. A new desk, too, with drawers for paper and pencils and markers. Jennifer even had her own matching bookcase. There were pictures and photographs in her room, Precious Moments figurines, Bible study notebooks. Everything gleamed, right down to the glass eyes on her stuffed animals, and Jennifer had dominion over it all. "Be careful," she said when I looked at her books. On a sheet of poster board she had stenciled flowers and curlicues, making a sign for her door: THE JENNIFER ZONE.

I was glad when she and her family flew off to Florida for a Disney World vacation. I had endured her gloating for weeks: the prospect of Epcot; how their hotel had two different swimming pools. While they were away, carpenters were finishing work on their screened-in back porch. The house was unlocked in the afternoons, and on the day before the Vander Wals' return, Anh and I broke in.

I don't remember how the idea formed, or who suggested it, but it was instant agreement and action. We didn't know what we were after. But we knew where we were headed, down the basement steps to the Jennifer Zone. As we moved in swift silence, I felt a heady, dizzying rush, the thrill of the trespass.

In Jennifer's room my sister opened the dresser drawers and balled up the clothes. She opened the closet and pushed every dress off its hanger. I went to Jennifer's desk and crumpled papers in my fist, then gently put them back. I threw her markers into the trash. Anh found a canister of baby powder and sprinkled it all over the room, dusting Jennifer's clothes and shoes, pulling back the bedcovers to get at the pillows and sheets. When she handed me the can I doused the desk drawers, the toy animals and dolls on the bed. We seemed to work in tandem, our focus methodical—there was so much, I realized, we could do.

At last Anh hissed that we should get out of there. We crept up the stairway and into the kitchen. Instead of hurrying out, I went toward the living room. Anh grabbed my shirt and shook her head—the workers were on the back porch, too close. But I had only one more thing to accomplish: I lifted the lid of the ceramic blue cookie jar. As I pulled out two cookies one of the workers said, "Did you hear something?" Anh and I flew out of the house and I put a cookie in my mouth. It was thick and heavy, Toll House chocolate chip.

The next night we got into the oversized T-shirts we used as pajamas and went to bed early. All day we had traded furtive glances, and I felt closer to her than I had in a long time. Together we had delivered payback for the funny looks, the polite no-thank-yous that signified, *You're different. You're strange. You people.* We had shown the Vander Wals they couldn't mess with us.

At the same time, though, the rush of satisfaction was edged with guilt. I did not hate Jennifer, who was my summer friend. But I hated, more and more, how I felt around her: how I dreamed of Shake 'n Bake; how she shook her head at the chilled lychees that Noi brought out to us on the hottest afternoons.

Rosa walked into the room, and the stony look on her face said it all.

"Well," she said. "The cat's out of the bag."

She made us go over to Jennifer's that night, in our T-shirts and flip-flops, and mumble apologies. We stood in the living room, our faces cast down, and in spite of the humiliation I couldn't help thinking how funny it was to be here at last, in the grown-ups' room, where company sat. It was the first time my parents had been in the house. The Vander Wals sat on the plaid sofa with round tufted pillows, and Linda prodded Jennifer to say in a princess voice, "I accept your apology."

As we shuffled back home, the dew slicking our ankles, Rosa told Anh and me that we could have gone to jail. My father said nothing. We were scared he was going to take out his belt and spank us something serious, but he didn't. Perhaps he felt bad for us; perhaps he understood what we had done better than we did.

Within a week Jennifer and I were back to normal, meaning

we both needed each other and resented each other, bound as we were by proximity and age. But for the first couple of days I stayed inside, afraid to face her. Jennifer had looked indignant the night of the apology, but there was something more: pity. I saw then that she had always pitied me and my unsaved soul.

In my grandmother's room I gazed up at the Buddha sitting on a high shelf. On a table below him lay arrangements of peaches, plums, and bananas; black-and-white photographs of my grandfather who died in 1956 and my uncle who died in the war; two urns filled with ashes. It calmed me to be in this room, to sit on the carpet and watch Noi light her favorite incense.

I went into the garage to dig out my bicycle and ride around the block a few times by myself. The garage was stifling and dim, and smelled of motor oil and dust. Here were broken mattresses, a pile of bricks and siding, rakes with missing tines. Sometimes, after drinking too much, my father would tell the story of how we had arrived here with five dollars. By *here* he meant America. Grand Rapids, Michigan. 1975. A world of cold and snow and people leaning down, saying, *What? What did you say?*

My apology to Jennifer had been for her room. No one had noticed the missing cookies, and my sister and I had said nothing. As I pedaled toward Sienna Street I cherished that secret. I knew the cookies would stay with me forever, echoing with each successive one I might eat and learn to make, each chocolate chip a reminder of the toll, the price of admission into a long-desired house. How I wanted such entrance through cookies, through candy and cake, popsicles, ice cream, endless kinds of dinner. I wanted all of it, and hated to be hungry.

6

School Lunch

THIRD GRADE AT KEN-O-SHA ELEMENTARY WAS LED BY Mrs. Andersen, an imperious woman who wore plaid skirts held tight with giant safety pins. She had a habit of twisting her wedding ring around and around her finger while she stood at the chalkboard. In Mrs. Andersen's classroom, good grades and behavior manifested themselves in star stickers—consolation green for effort, gold for highest achievement—accumulating on a large board that loomed over us all. One glance and you could see who was behind and who was striding ahead. The percentage grades on homework assignments translated easily, but Mrs. Andersen had total control of the good behavior stars; in her cryptic system, one day you might get a gold and the next, demoted to silver.

In pursuit of gold stars I became an insufferably good student, with perfect Palmer cursive and one hundred percents in every subject. I had something to prove—to myself, to Mrs. Andersen, to everyone in the class.

At home, when my parents exhibited some of the typical immigrant strictness about grades, Crissy and Anh, as the older siblings, bore much of the burden. I saw my father glowering at their report cards, holding them like garbage scraps as he asked, "Why aren't these better?" If Anh got an A-minus on an assignment he would say "Where's the A?" Good grades weren't praised; they were expected. While I was spurred to distinguish myself from my sisters, mostly I was just a natural-born nerd. (However, I couldn't fulfill Rosa's great wish for me: to become a classical violinist like the graceful Asian prodigies she saw on TV.)

The trick I had learned was that the quieter I was, and the better I was in school, the more the teacher would let me alone. I might have aimed for middle-of-the-road, the blend-in average student. But my need for approval in the classroom overrode everything else. The good students had privileges, after all: they could escape notice; they could even do independent study at the back of the room or out in the hallway. Being good meant freedom from watchfulness.

The worst thing was being called on or in any way standing out more than I already did in a class that was, except for me, one other Vietnamese immigrant, and one black student, dough-white. If, in the dreaded reading circle, I was told to read out loud, Mrs. Andersen would interrupt me, snapping, "You're reading too fast!" "Speak up! Louder!"

Privately I admired the rebellious kids, like Robbie Wilson, who always wore an old jean jacket, even in the winter, and would come to school looking bleary-eyed and pinched, like an adult with a hangover. Robbie and his ilk talked back at teachers, got sent to the principal's office, and were even spanked with the principal's infamous red paddle. These kids refused to settle down or do what they were told. They possessed what seemed to me marvelous nerve and self-knowledge, allowing them to question everything. During PE, when the gym teacher led us in aerobics to a song called "Go You Chicken Fat, Go!" they sang, "Go you chicken shit, go!"

On our first foray in school my sister and I had encountered kids who laughed and pointed at us, pressing back the edges of their eyes with their palms while they chanted, "Ching-chong, ching chong!" At first I didn't understand what those noises meant. Ching-chong? For *me*? I saw how the other kids, the different, black-haired ones, stared at the ground or ran away. "Chop suey!" white kids would yell. "Hi-*ya*!" I was afraid to ask my parents what "chop suey" was; they had yelled at me when I had asked what "bitch" meant. So it wasn't until a few years later, when I saw a can of La Choy at Meijer Thrifty Acres, that I understood, and wondered at being called a mix of noodles and vegetables.

At home, on warm days after rain when toadstools bloomed in our yard, my grandmother went to dig them up. When the kids in the neighborhood saw this they screwed up their faces. "Are you gonna eat them for supper?" they called out, laughing, their Kool-Aid mouths wide. My sister dealt with the matter by telling them that they'd get a knuckle sandwich if they didn't shut up—and made good on it. I did not have Anh's fierceness and glow; I became self-conscious to the point of being, at times, unable to speak. Words like *stranger* and *funny-looking* ran loose in my mind.

At Ken-O-Sha, whatever academic success I had was completely eroded at lunchtime. Here, a student was measured by the contents of her lunch bag, which displayed status, class, and parental love. I didn't tell anyone that I packed my own lunch, but the girls in my grade figured it out. "My mom *loves* to pack my lunch," said Sara Jonkman, whose hard blue eyes emitted a vicious spark.

The anxiety of what to pack weighed on me every school week. The key was to have at least one shining element: a plain sandwich and baggie of potato chips could be made tolerable with the right dessert snack. If the planets and grocery sales aligned in my favor, I might even have a Hostess Cupcake. All morning I would look forward to peeling away the flat layer of deep chocolate frosting decorated with one lovely white squiggle. This I set aside while I ate the cake, licking out the cream filling, sighing over the richness, the darkness of the crumbs. Then at last I could focus on the frosting, taking small bites around the white squiggle, which must always be saved as long as possible. I imagined careful bakers hovering over each cupcake, forming the curlicue design with unerring precision. Beneath the status of Hostess Cupcakes were Ho Hos, Ding Dongs, Devil Squares, Zingers, and Little Debbie Fudge Brownies. The lower tier, just above generic cookies, included the cloying Oatmeal Creme Pies, SnoBalls, Star Crunches, and Twinkies.

Not long after third grade started I ditched my banged-up Scooby-Doo lunch box, which smelled faintly of deli meat no matter how much I washed it, for the brown paper bags that everyone else was using. Luckily they were inexpensive, so my stepmother didn't object to buying them. The bags provided little protection for my sandwiches, which always got smushed before lunch hour. Rosa bought whatever white bread was cheapest— sadly, never the Wonder Bread my friends ate, which I was certain had a fluffier, more luxurious bite—and peanut butter and jelly, olive loaf, or thin packets of pastrami and corned beef made by a company called Buddig. The name drove me crazy, the way it sounded like a stuffed-up nose, and I wanted to rewrite every package to make it Budding.

Whenever Rosa got sick of buying lunch items she signed me and my sisters up for the school lunch. She was always angling to get them for free, but our family fell just above the qualifying level. This relieved me to no end; everyone knew about the kids who got free lunches because their names were on a separate checklist.

Each month a new lunch menu was posted on a bulletin board outside the gym-cafeteria. Reading it over and over, to the point of memorization, became one of my pastimes.

> Grilled cheese sandwich
> Fried chicken
> Whipped potatoes and gravy
> Choice of corn or peas
> Fruit cup

Their words sent me dreaming; every day seemed a promise. Most provocative were listings that mentioned choice, the word itself conjuring possibility: "choice of hamburger or cheeseburger"; "choice of whole milk or chocolate milk." In reality, hot lunch meant soggy cheese sandwiches encased in steamed-up plastic pouches; perforated boxes of greasy, chewy fried chicken; elastic potatoes; canned fruit in heavy syrup. Still, I imagined potatoes churned into clouds and slicked with gravy, served alongside the mysterious but elegant-sounding Salisbury steak.

I knew better than to admit this fascination to anyone. School lunch was unanimously described as gross, for one thing, save for the passable rectangles of cheese pizza that sometimes appeared;

any cold lunch was preferable to the degradation of styrofoam meal trays bearing fish sticks and baked beans. The implicit judgment was that if you had to get lunch from the cafeteria, then your mom obviously didn't care enough.

No one cared more than Holly Jansen's mom.

In the middle of the school year Holly started bringing her lunch in a tomato-red Tupperware container. It might have been totally not cool except for the fact that beautiful Melinda Smith, who ruled our class with her electric-blue eyes and spun-gold hair, finer than anyone else's in the entire school, also started bringing her lunch in a Tupperware container. These items, I learned, were not only expensive but rare. One had to know someone to get them. One had to be invited to purchase them.

I watched as Holly unlatched the Tupperware and drew from it her first course: a sandwich wrapped like a gift in wax paper. Holly's sandwiches were never limp or squashed, battered by books in a schoolbag. They were fresh and white, cut into matching rectangles. Slices of bologna did not hang carelessly over the bread; smudges of peanut butter and jelly did not mar the crust. After Holly ate her sandwich, mindful that crumbs did not fall on her clothes, she pulled out her second course, the one that always got to me: SpaghettiOs or Campbell's chicken noodle soup kept hot in a thermos, or a square of Jeno's pizza sliced into bite-sized pieces. The rest—Hi-C juice box, chocolate chip cookies—hardly mattered in comparison to the SpaghettiOs drowning in orange sauce, or the pizza that became, in Holly's hands, refined.

Such poise came to her as naturally as her powder-blue eyes and hair curled just so at her shoulders. Her wardrobe of monogrammed sweaters and lace-trimmed socks seemed to arrive straight from Rogers Department Store's back-to-school billboards. All the Hostess cupcakes in Grand Rapids couldn't measure up to what Holly had. I pictured a spacious kitchen, sunlit and Clorox clean, Mrs. Jansen standing at the counter tucking each lunch component into the Tupperware. Some days, she would slip a little note between the cookies and thermos. *Hope you're having a great day! Love, Mom.*

Holly and I had become friendly because we had the best cursive in the class and were thus allowed to study quietly in the hallway while the other kids practiced their handwriting. From there we started playing together at recess and sitting together at lunch. One day she broke off a corner of her mother's banana bread and presented it to me. The taste filled my mouth with a nutty, sweet spice I wanted to capture again and again. I would never have dared to ask for more, but as our friendship increased so did her sharing: a sliver of pizza, a morsel of blueberry muffin, half a chocolate chip cookie.

At Halloween, Holly could be counted on to have a good costume: she'd be a cat with painted-on whiskers, wearing a store-bought costume that came with a headband of cat ears and a fuzzy tail. Or she'd be a princess with a tall cone-shaped hat that spilled a length of tulle around her hair. I had conflicted feelings about Halloween. The joy of free candy was mitigated by my homemade, pieced-together costumes; there was no pleasure in disguise when it only made people ask, "What are you supposed to be?" My parents thought spending money on costumes was ridiculous, so we would dress up as hobos or punk rockers. Once, Rosa borrowed someone's mortarboard and gown and sent me off trick-or-treating as a graduate. I would console my-

self by organizing my piles of candy and ranking them according to desirability (dead last were Necco wafers and the nameless
peanut butter candies that came wrapped in orange or black
paper).

Holly thought it wild that my siblings and I were allowed to
trick-or-treat by ourselves after dark. She went with her parents
around dusk, carrying a bag shaped like a jack-o'-lantern. I didn't
tell her that we carried pillowcases shucked from our beds. Holly
existed on a different plane; I believed if I offended her sensi-
bilities, she might recoil from me in disgust. I don't know if
she knew how fascinated I was by her impeccable manners—
she never spilled, never stumbled, never crumpled paper napkins
into balls. At age eight she seemed to me a practically full-grown
person, completely sure of herself, confident of each bite she took,
each step she made in the world.

Two years later Holly would fulfill a homework assignment—
"Report on a Natural Phenomenon"—by describing how her
mother made banana bread: how she stirred the ingredients together; how she bent to put the loaf pan in the oven. Holly
watched the bread rise and grow brown and delicious-smelling.
But the bread, it turned out, came from a Jiffy mix. Her blueberry
muffins, too. When I heard that, I entreated my stepmother to
buy me some Jiffy mix—it was about forty cents a box—swearing
that I could follow the directions. Tired and annoyed, she gave
in. Those Jiffy muffins, studded with artificial blueberries, baked
up golden and petite, just like the pictures on the box. Laying the
muffin tin on the stovetop, I marveled at their exactness and felt
relief, a little mean gladness that I was finally able to have what

Holly had every day. But the muffins didn't taste the same as her mother's. They were ordinary, far from a phenomenon. They were missing the element no one in my family could supply.

One night, years later when I was in college, I drove to Chelsea, Michigan, to see the home of the Jiffy Corporation. The giant Jiffy grain hotel faced me from the middle of Main Street. It towered, monstrous, creamy white, surrounded by a wisp of chain-link fence. As I crossed an empty lot toward it the word "Jiffy," bright blue and serifed with its trademark quotation marks, expanded. I remembered so clearly the taste of those blueberry muffins, of Mrs. Jansen's banana bread, and I stopped walking. I didn't know where I was going. I imagined the grain hotel filled with muffin mix, all those dried blueberries stifled in flour and sugar. The town was quiet and small, hushed but for the hum of electricity and this building, its sustaining presence. Something about the moment filled me with fear—as if the grain hotel would fall down, smother and erase me.

In the gold-star race I was neck and neck with Holly and Melanie, a towheaded girl with heavy bangs and endearingly large feet. My behavior stars weren't as great as theirs, but my homework stars shined just as bright. Toward the middle of third grade Mrs. Andersen introduced a stuffed lion to the reward system: each week the best student, the one with the most gold stars, would earn the privilege of having the lion sit on her desk. How I craved that stuffed lion! He was tawny and plump, with a mane like a sunflower wreath. But week after week the lion went to Holly's desk or Melanie's desk.

Meanwhile, the class spelling bee came, and it threw me into conflict: on the one hand I hated everyone watching me; on the other hand I wanted to be the best. And I loved spelling. It came easily to me, part of my obsessive need to know the right words for things. When I won the spelling bee I accepted the prizes—a scalloped-edged certificate and a Mr. Goodbar—with a relief and pride that transcended my usual reticence. That afternoon as I started toward home I remembered that I'd forgotten my rain boots in my locker. I doubled back to school and overheard Mrs. Andersen in the classroom talking to another teacher. "Can you believe it?" she was saying. "A foreigner winning our spelling bee!"

I waited for the stuffed lion the rest of that year, but he never did perch at the edge of my desk. In June, on the last day of school, Mrs. Andersen gave the lion to Holly to keep forever.

The next year, when Vinh started kindergarten, Anh was in fifth grade and I in fourth. We walked him to school each morning and took turns taking him back home at lunchtime. I liked the in-charge feeling of being an older sister, and during our walks I made him listen to a long story I made up as I went along, each installment ending with "to be continued." The story started with a boy and meandered through forests, meadows, and castles— there were wicked enemies and wise animals, kindnesses and violence, triumphs and tests, royal banquets with heaps of food. Vinh endured this patiently, remembering characters I'd abandoned, at times pointing out a storyline I'd already used. He was a happy, thoughtful five-year-old, generous with his time and toys. If he had a candy bar he would split it with me right down the middle. I often envied his birth and automatic U.S. citizenship (he could run for president someday, Rosa pointed out), which seemed to confer upon him an ease of mind, or so I imagined. But mostly I felt protective, for he was regarded as a gift by everyone in the family. The youngest one. The only son. The only child of my father and Rosa.

While none of my siblings seemed to feel the intense shyness that wore me out daily, Vinh at least also lacked the toughness that Anh and Crissy had. They had fierceness, the kind that didn't need to find expression in good behavior and careful cursive; if we played Office with them they would always be the bosses. And Vinh was a little boy, exempt from the anxieties of wanting to look pretty, something else my sisters had already conquered. Taking on the role of older sister allowed me some release from myself, allowed me to throw off the mantle of classroom self-consciousness and not mind so much, because Vinh didn't, the thick, chunky-framed glasses I was cursed to wear.

Traipsing home in the winter, my brother and I pretended to be explorers. We took shortcuts through the block to see if we could walk on backyards of iced-over snow or if our weight would send us crashing through to the ground. As soon as we got home we yanked our moon boots off inside out and left them in a damp pile. We never washed our hands or bothered with napkins. We raced each other to the kitchen counter for bowls of shrimp-flavored *mi* soup, sliced steaks seared with onion and garlic, and french fries that soaked up the juices from the meat. Noi would keep frying the potatoes as we ate, sliding them onto our plates. All the while, an extra serving sat at the dining table for the spirits of our ancestors. Their food was always cold by the time Noi ate it for her own lunch. She would wrap the potatoes in lettuce and dip them in vinegar. Afterward, she whittled us apple wedges or cut a cantaloupe into bite-sized pieces. *Ngon quá!* Vinh and I exclaimed, our voices tilting up on the second-syllable accent. *So delicious!* We were safe for a while, cocooned in Noi's kitchen, and at such times I never missed my friends in the cafeteria.

Before heading back to school I followed Noi back to her bedroom, where she would watch her afternoon lineup of *Days of Our Lives* and *Another World* on the television Chu Cuong had given her. I loved the calmness that radiated from Buddha, positioned on his high shelf, while the oranges clustered below him grew ripe with waiting. Noi settled on her bed with her knitting bag and Vinh gathered his books for the afternoon. I always wanted to stay with them, skip out on the rest of school, admire the tenderness of Bo and Hope and drowse in the warmth from the radiator. But I never did. Mindful of gold stars and how they stretched across the classroom, I hurried back to Ken-O-Sha, taking the shortcut so as not to be late.

7

American Meat

I WAS NINE WHEN I LEARNED HOW TO USE A KNIFE. Everything my grandmother cooked or fed us came in bite-size pieces, whether in a bowl of fruit or a plate of stir-fry, so there was never any need to know how to cut a T-bone steak. But I pretended to know American meat as well as anybody: prime rib, pork chops, meat loaf. If the girls at recess talked about these things that they had eaten the night before I would simply chime in, "Me, too."

By the beginning of fourth grade Holly Jansen and I had become BFF, best friends forever, and she made it official by inviting me for a sleepover. I never would have invited her to my house. I didn't have my own room, for one thing. And I was afraid, both of how my family would act around Holly and how she would react to being around them. I could imagine her startled glance at Buddha and the altar for the ancestors. I had already seen Jennifer Vander Wal shrink away from it. If Holly came over, she would have to eat my grandmother's strange food for dinner; she would have to deal with everyone talking over the TV and the barking dog. I knew such things didn't happen in other households. Almost none of the kids I knew, in all of my school years in Grand Rapids, had any cats or dogs. It was some kind of Dutch obsession with cleanliness, Rosa said, some hatred of things other than human.

On the day of the sleepover I rode the bus home with Holly. She lived in a subdivision called Princeton Estates, which was about the fanciest name I'd ever heard. Her house rose up two stories, with tan vinyl siding and a prominent two-stall garage in front. Inside was as pristine as the Vander Wals' house and smelled the same—faint reminders of clean laundry, Lysol, and early morning baking. It was apparent that the real mothers in Grand Rapids knew exactly how to run a house, how it should look and smell. They were in on some code that my stepmother had been left out of. Their rooms possessed remarkable calm, as if no one had ever raised a voice there. Arguments didn't happen; chaos never ensued. The house was free of all bacteria, dirt, and excess noise. I felt that I could lie down and sleep comfortably, forever, on the creamy carpet that blanketed the second floor. The look-but-don't-touch living room had fresh vacuum marks on the same pale carpet, and a grandfather clock ticked in one corner. The sofas were plaid, to match the drapes, and bore pillows that Holly's mother had cross-stitched.

On the outside Holly and I were polar opposites: she was tall, blond, and kempt; I was short, black-haired, with clothes that knew no iron. In some ways my friendship with Holly was another version of the one I had with Jennifer Vander Wal, but instead of resentful envy I mostly felt admiration. Holly and I were drawn to each other not just by proximity but by our shared desire to be orderly and perfect. To me Holly had already achieved this through her inherent being, but maybe she didn't believe it.

We both worked so hard to be good. Teachers often let us study in the hallway by ourselves—advanced reading or independent math, they called it. But once in the hallway Holly and I played word games and devised an elaborate *Wheel of Fortune* board. We were also the only ones in our class whose parents voted Democrat. The following year, in the weeks leading up to the 1984 presidential election, the other kids would stand together in the courtyard at recess and chant, "Reagan! Reagan!" In response Holly and I alone would feebly call out, "Mondale, Mondale!"

The closer Holly and I became, the more I wanted to be like her. On the day of the sleepover I felt light-headed with nervousness; I was terrified of disappointing her, of making a mistake that would show the low errors of my upbringing and very self. Looking in the mirror every morning before school I wondered why I could not be transformed. If only my hair, at the very least, would cooperate and look like Holly's, bending into a soft curl at the shoulder. Instead my hair fell bluntly, as if cleaver-chopped, laced with wintertime static.

In Holly's house her mother greeted us with a snack of banana bread and milk, which we ate carefully in the breakfast nook. How was school? Mrs. Jansen wanted to know. Did we have any special homework assignments for the weekend? She cleaned as she talked, wiping down the spotless counters and scrubbing the sink. With her hair trimmed into a practical, motherly-looking bob, she was by all appearances Holly's clear and desired future. As I watched her work in the kitchen I searched for clues and answers to How Things Were Supposed to Be.

Once, playing on the merry-go-round at recess, Holly asked me if I had a real mother. She had met Rosa at our school play and didn't understand why I called her my mom. I told her my real mother was in Vietnam. When Holly asked why, I lied, "She likes it there better." I didn't add that I had never met her, that I didn't know her name or what she looked like. Holly mulled over my reply. "Did your mom and dad get divorced?" she wanted to know. I said yes. It sounded like a plausible enough explanation, and it became the story I told all of my friends from then on, if they asked.

Holly's bedroom was done up in yellow and white gingham, with coordinating window valances and ruffled bed skirt. Not a wrinkle marred the neatly made bed, where glassy-eyed dolls and stuffed animals, including the coveted lion from Mrs. Andersen's class, sat posed as though for a portrait. A bulletin board above Holly's desk displayed Field Day ribbons (she was a good runner and natural athlete) and family pictures. Out in the hallway, I got a glimpse into her parents' bedroom. Two twin beds covered in identical green blankets. I was about to ask Holly why—my parents slept in one big bed—but something made me keep the question in check.

Holly and I spent all afternoon playing in the finished basement, which was decked out with two complete offices—one for Holly and one for her older sister Sandra. Our favorite game was, in fact, Office. We played secretaries. We aspired to secretary status. The words *executive secretary* and *legal secretary* swelled our vocabulary and hearts. We wrote memos, phone messages, reports. Other times we played waitress, taking imaginary families' elaborate orders, because we aspired to that job as well. The menu items were all Holly's: prime rib, fried chicken, baked potatoes, corn, and she had Legos and figurines to represent each dish.

Meanwhile, upstairs, Holly's mother was "getting dinner." After a while I detected the scent of roasting meat, and as the smell grew stronger I grew more anxious. How would I know how to act at dinner? What would I say to Holly's parents? What if I spilled on myself?

When Holly heard the mechanical sound of the garage door opening she jumped up, exclaiming, "My dad's home!" She ran upstairs and I followed her. I felt vaguely homesick, tired. I hadn't celebrated my father's return from work since the days on Baldwin Street when he would toss my sister and me in the air. Now I avoided his arrival, staying put in Noi's closet with my books and stolen desserts. When he came home with a dark face and callused hands, tired of machinery, even Vinh knew to tiptoe around him. Rosa meanwhile shuttled between her ESL work downtown and her classes at Grand Valley State, where she was earning her master's in education. Coming back from school, she usually found my father sitting on the backyard patio, no matter how cold it was, smoking Winston after Winston.

Holly's father was balding and spectacled. With his navy-blue sport jacket, striped tie, and polished cordovan shoes, he looked just like fathers and businessmen on TV. It didn't matter what kind of business. The important thing was that he did something quiet and white collar, in an office, something that commanded respect. He came home from work clean.

"Hello," he said in a kind voice. I never knew if it carried generosity or pity. As he spoke to his daughters and wife the word *cozy* ran though my mind. It was a word I'd gleaned from *The Boxcar Children* and *Little Women*. I wanted cozy, and I wanted this. People who spoke softly and nicely! Who never looked rumpled, hair all out of place! Dinner as an event!

"Let's wash up," Holly directed. I washed my hands as if I did so every day and followed my friend to the dinner table. It was set the way mine at home never was, with floral place mats, tumblers filled with ice water, and matching silverware. A knot of fear struck me as I surveyed it all. At home my parents had taken to using paper plates for every meal, tucking them into wicker paper plate holders that became encrusted with dried bits of food. On weekdays we ate our meals on our own. Noi would cook in the afternoons, keeping the food warm and the rice fresh in its cooker for whenever we got home from school.

On the Jansens' dinner table there were bowls of peas, applesauce, and potatoes whipped with an electric mixer. These circled the core, the main event: a wide platter of meat. At least, I knew it was meat, but I couldn't tell much more than that. The slabs were grayish brown, thick with bone, and daunting.

As if reading my mind Holly said, "Pork chops." She spoke the words reverently.

Holly's sister came into the dining room. "Please have a seat," she said, smiling like her mother. Sandra was two years older and had her own quiet interests—piano lessons, Sunday School, studying. Like Holly, she favored pastel crewneck sweaters over white turtlenecks. A gold necklace peeked out from in between.

At the table everyone bowed their heads and Holly's father said a prayer. I bowed my head, too. My religious rebellion against Jennifer Vander Wal and her acolytes had held fast, so I only pretended to pray, grateful for a moment to pull myself together. But I also felt like a fraud, not because of prayer but because the ritual was so intimate, so much theirs and not mine. I was a squatter, an imposter. A ruiner of other people's family dinners.

At the "amen" everyone looked up and smiled. I noticed that they had all set their napkins in their laps. I followed their lead, though it mystified me. At home, I kept napkins balled up next to my plate for easy access.

Holly's mother began passing the bowls around and I copied whatever Holly did. She took a large spoonful of peas and dropped a dollop of applesauce on her plate. I did the same. She forked a large pork chop in the middle of it all and I tried to do the same, but the meat stuck to the fork. A wave of panic came over me just before Holly's father intervened, gently helping the pork chop slide onto the home base of my plate.

Mr. Jansen asked Sandra about her school day. Then he asked Holly and me, but I was too nervous to respond. Perhaps Holly sensed it, because she did all of the talking. I needed all my concentration to get through the meal. I watched the others, uncertain about the applesauce. It was something Rosa sometimes bought in huge jars, when they were on sale, to have as dessert. The Jansens wielded their knives and forks expertly as they carved out bites of pork chop. They dredged each piece in applesauce and deposited the whole into their mouths, never spilling a drop. From there they made the rounds of potatoes and peas, circling back to the pork.

I thought of weekend afternoons when my family gathered together for Noi's *pho*, well simmered with oxtail, onions, and star anise. She prepared each bowl individually, ladling thin slices of beef into the vat of broth until they were just cooked, then releasing them onto a mound of noodles. On the table there were plates piled with herbs, bean sprouts, and lime wedges, jars of hoisin and Sriracha, and a dish of sliced hot chilies. When my father, uncles, and Noi ate *pho* they leaned in close to the bowls, sniffing deeply to take in the deep, delicate fragrance of the soup.

Then they fell to eating, using chopsticks to loop up skeins of noodles and suck them into their mouths, and Chinese spoons to slurp the broth. Having dinner with the Jansens, I realized how much noise, how much of a mess, everyone in my family made. We chomped down big mouthfuls of food, splashed the table and ourselves, snatched sprigs of coriander with our hands. We spiced our soups until our tongues burned, our foreheads glazed with sweat. At the end of the meal my father would go into the kitchen and fish out a beef bone from the bottom of the pot, aiming for every last bit of marrow.

At Holly's house I picked up the knife and fork, grasping them the way she did. I planted the fork into the graying wedge of meat, making sure I had a good grip. But cutting the meat wasn't as easy as it looked. The pork was tough, and I couldn't figure out where the bone was exactly, or how to maneuver around it. My heart pounding, I continued sawing away. I began to feel some progress, some give. Inside, the meat was a duller gray, and dry straight through.

When the knife pushed through the final barrier of flesh and hit the plate, it made the sound that ice skates make when a skater slices into a jump. The stub of meat, cleaved free of its chop, sailed through the air and dropped onto the carpet near Mr. Jansen's chair.

Hands shaking, face burning, I set my knife and fork down. I eyed the fallen meat with terror—a stain on the carpet, on my entire being. I would have given anything for my family dog, Mimi, to be there to snap up the evidence. I didn't know what to do: retrieve the meat? Say something? All around me the eating continued. No one at the table said a word or in any way registered what had happened. A moment later Holly's father reached down and picked up the meat with his napkin. He did this so swiftly it seemed an act of magic, my transgression erased from the family table.

Somehow, I made it through the rest of that dinner, even managing to get a couple bites of the remaining pork chop. The meat was gristly and fatty, starkly unspiced. I chewed hard, chasing it down with the potatoes and applesauce. I did not speak a word.

Back at home, Rosa shuddered at the idea of pork and applesauce, going so far as to say, "Yucko." In truth I was relieved to be at home again, to have the beef sliced into easy pieces in the salty stew, to see half-inch squares of tofu bobbing in a clear soup. But the lesson hard-learned at Holly's stayed with me. I would never endure that panic again. To make sure, I began practicing with a knife and fork. I cut small pieces of chicken stir-fry into even smaller pieces. I hacked up stalks of bok choy and Chinese broccoli, and curried eggs. At lunch Noi served up the usual ramen, steak, and fries, but stopped cutting the meat for me. She didn't say anything about it but left out a knife and fork so I could attack the beef.

One day Rosa saw me practicing and said, "You know, only Americans do that. *Europeans* eat differently." That got my attention, for she knew how enamored I was of all things British: Mary Poppins, Charles Dickens, names like Margaret and Elizabeth. She demonstrated how to slice off a piece of meat and eat it without switching the fork from one hand to the other. "Americans don't know how to eat truly correctly, the way Europeans do." She gave me a smile I couldn't interpret—part sad, part reluctant.

So I practiced both methods, saving them up for an imagined future.

8

Green Sticky Rice Cakes

BEFORE I STARTED SCHOOL, MY CONCEPT OF THE world was largely formed by TV shows. Making friends on the playground would be like *Charlie's Angels*, I imagined. Or maybe *Laverne & Shirley*, with me wearing a big cursive *B* on every outfit. Anh and I sometimes practiced marching down the street, arm in arm, shouting our own mangled version of *Schlemeel, Schlemazel, Hasenfeffer Incorporated!* The delusion that I could become Laverne or Shirley, Janet from *Three's Company*, or Vicki, the *Love Boat* captain's daughter, stayed with me through most of my kindergarten year at Chamberlain Elementary. Rosa had enrolled Anh and me there because it had a bilingual education program that she was certain we needed. As soon as we learned enough English, she said, we could transfer to nearby Ken-O-Sha.

The bus to Chamberlain Elementary stopped at the corner of Florence and Sienna Streets, and as Anh and I waited there in the frosty mornings we could see our grandmother Noi sitting on the front stoop, watching until the bus arrived. I never saw Noi sleeping and I never saw her rushing. She moved with smooth, even steps, measured by some internal metronome. On school days she made sure that Anh and I were planted at the corner of the street well before the bus arrived, instilling in us such a great fear of missing school that I often had nightmares about it. When school let out we would tear across the yard, worrying that the bus would take off without us.

I liked my kindergarten teacher, Mrs. Walter, a thin, wrinkly faced woman who wore bright orange lipstick. When she learned that I and a couple of other girls already knew how to read, she let us sit in a corner with our books while the other kids played with memory cards and built fortresses out of Loc Blocs. I became fast friends with Corinne, who was black, wore ribbons in her hair, and was just my size: small and rounded, with a mischievous look on her face. Side by side, we read Sweet Pickles books, opened a field guide to birds and decided which ones were our favorites. Corinne liked cardinals and I liked bluebirds, but we agreed on the beauty of the scarlet tanager. As the year wore on we practiced writing on sheets of beige lined paper that Mrs. Walter gave us, copying words from books. We rejoined the rest of the class for snack time—Ritz crackers spread with peanut butter—and sing-along. Sitting at an old upright piano, Mrs. Walter would play "Puff the Magic Dragon" and "I'd Like to Teach the World to Sing in Perfect Harmony."

Kindergarten was the last good time I had in school.

The next year, I had to join Anh in bilingual education class. Three times a week we were excused from our regular classrooms to meet Mr. Ho and Miss Huong in a conference room near the principal's office. They hovered over a growing band of newer Vietnamese students, most of them older than Anh and I, some who'd had their ages changed on their green card paperwork so they could start school at a lower grade. They studied their workbooks intently. By comparison, Anh and I were completely Americanized. We also knew English as well as any of the white kids, but we kept that fact between ourselves. We were girls who did what we were told, and if Rosa said we needed bilingual education then we went along. I remember mimeographs from English language guide books, the purple ink smudging my hands. Mr. Ho and Miss Huong led us through exercise drills: *How are you? I am fine, thank you. Thank you for the directions. Teacher, may I please use the bathroom?* I felt silly, a fraud, but I chanted the words anyway, pretending to learn.

My regular first-grade teacher, Mrs. Sikkema, had hair like a shower cap and a sour, pinched face. She always assessed homework with a drawing of a ghost. *Good job!* And then a loopy Casper, smiling. Anh, now happily ensconced in gentle Mrs. Hanley's second grade, had warned me about Mrs. Sikkema's grouchiness. When the time came for me to slink off to bilingual ed she would throw a cold look my way, and all the other students would look, too. That's when I became friends with Loan, the other Vietnamese girl in first grade. At recess we stuck together, for it was during one of these breaks that we first encountered a group of kids yelling at us while they pushed their eyelids into slits. Lowering our heads to conceal our faces and eyes, we hurried away. We played with Corinne and Lucy, a freckled, curly-haired girl who had lost half of her left arm to an accident. The playground had huge cement tubes to crawl through and balance on, and sometimes the four of us sat huddled together inside, looking at the graffiti the older kids had scrawled on the walls: a litany of names, hearts, and stars.

Once, out of nowhere, a pale girl with frizzy pigtails tied with pink ribbons challenged me to a fight on the playground.

She appeared toward the end of recess as I was jumping off a swing. Wearing a tight jumper and a hooded coat, she faced me squarely, her eyes gray as the sky. She might have been a third- or fourth-grader. I had never seen her before. "Come on," she said, balling up her hands into fists. "Let's fight." I looked at Corinne and Lucy, who stood frozen. Pigtails' friends took a couple of steps forward and one of them halfheartedly pointed to Corinne and said, "I guess we should fight, too."

It had rained earlier that day, and the whole playground still smelled like worms. I thought about what it would feel like to get punched for real—not the fake way my sisters did—and how muddy my coat would get.

"Come on," Pigtails said, her fists at chin level.

"Okay," I replied. In spite of my terror, I had a clear sense that running away wouldn't work here. "Let me tie my shoes first," I said. I knelt down, scrunching myself up so Pigtails wouldn't see how slowly I tied and untied the laces. All of the girls waited. I kept tying the laces, drawing the moments out until the end-of-recess bell rang.

Corinne, Lucy, and I raced back to first grade and didn't speak of the incident. For months I kept a low profile at recess, afraid that the girl with the pigtails would seek me out, but I never saw her again. She had grown bored, I hoped, had moved on to someone else or forgotten me. Or perhaps I had gotten my wish and become invisible to her.

The first Tet festivities I remember happened that school year. The Vietnamese Community Center organized a day of festivities at the Marriott Hotel, a precursor to today's "celebration of diversity and multiculturalism." My stepmother, never one to be left out, got into the spirit by volunteering Anh and me to help showcase Tet at Chamberlain Elementary. She also signed me up to perform a traditional spring dance with seven other girls at the Marriott. When I complained, she told me that it was my duty. "It's your custom," she reminded me. "It's the way Vietnamese do things." She added that my father would be proud of me for dancing, a surefire way to get me to agree.

In the music room at Chamberlain we practiced dancing with the instructor, a young woman who was a friend of Miss Huong's. Loan and I were partners in the dance, and we giggled as we circled each other, tapping lightly on the paper drums that hung around our necks. Miss Huong didn't like it when I held the drum up to my chin, pretending to be a Saint Bernard like the ones I had seen in cartoons. She made Loan and me learn to pause, do a semi-curtsy, then weave around the other girls. The drums were yellow, and striped with red to mimic the Vietnamese flag. The real flag, my stepmother reminded me, not the evil Communist flag.

Rosa had a lot to say about Communists. They became a great tool for keeping us kids in line. "If you don't behave," she would warn, "the Communists are going to come get you. You know what they do? They march down the street, hundreds and thousands of them, and they take everyone from their houses." I would shiver, hearing her descriptions. "If the Communists take over we'll live in a police state," she said.

"What's a police state?" I asked.

"It's when you can't even go outside because they might shoot you."

I vaguely understood that "the Communists" were the reason

we had ended up in America, in Michigan. I knew that Communists had warred against the good guys—people like us. But no one explained why or what it all meant. In our household, the "why" question got me exactly nowhere. "Why are the Communists out to get us?" "Because they're bad." "Why are they bad?" "Because they're Communists." "Why?" "Because I said so."

Tet was a great holiday because it was all about food, firecrackers, and cash. My father and uncles would throw strings of snaps on the ground and hand out sparklers, rousing the ire and suspicion of the Vander Wals, which only goaded them on. But the first thing we did when we woke up was race to Noi and yell, *Chuc mung nam moi!* Happy New Year! As soon as we said it she would hand us little red envelopes stamped in gold and filled with fresh twenty-dollar bills.

Noi spent days preparing for Tet, and long before we got up she would have arranged a feast before Buddha. First, the labor-intensive *banh chung*, green sticky rice cakes steamed in banana leaves, tied with strips of bamboo and embellished with red ribbon. *Banh chung* could take two days to make: the sticky rice, the green beans mashed into a paste, the marinated pork. All of these had to be folded together in the right proportion for each cake, encased in banana or bamboo leaves, and tied into square bundles. As the cakes steamed, the green of the leaves seeped into the rice, turning it a lovely shade of celadon. *Banh chung* was a symbol of Tet—its painstaking effort, its presentation as a gift. When we ate these cakes we were supposed to honor the beginning of a new year of hopes and good wishes.

Everyone loved *banh chung* except me. Oh, I loved the packaging of it. I loved opening the smooth bamboo leaves to reveal the green glutinous rice beneath. But I never needed much more after the first bite—the rice clotted the roof of my mouth, the dusty bean paste got in the way of the treasured pork. Usually I gave the rest of my *banh chung* to Anh, who could eat them one after the other without stopping. I had a more fickle palate, easily bored, and wanted the crisp, oil-edged taste of *cha gio* (with plenty more ready to be fried in the kitchen), fresh *goi cuon* summer rolls, egg pancakes stuffed with herbs and bean sprouts, shrimp chips, fried shrimp, pickled carrots and shallots, fresh *bun* noodles topped with seasoned beef, coriander, and a fine sprinkling of peanuts, and doughy white *banh bao* balls stuffed with sweet Chinese sausage.

The Tet of 1981 seemed to last for days. Noi sewed matching *ao dais* for me and Anh out of a silky red fabric and white flowy pants. Rosa made us wear them to school, though we desperately did not want to, knowing how the other kids would stare at us. But it was Tet day, and there would be an assembly in the gym so that all the kids in the school could learn about the lunar new year. So we resigned ourselves: we would be on display.

Noi had made an extra pile of *banh chung* for Anh and me to take to school. The cakes appeared glimmering on a tin platter in the morning, tied with extra curled red ribbons, and well wrapped in plastic to keep them from drying out. Because we were dressed in our *ao dais* our teachers assumed we would be spending the morning preparing for the assembly. We didn't correct them. The feeling of being set apart in our outfits had united us. Alone we were self-conscious, but together we were emboldened. So instead of going to bilingual class, or to the gym where boys were practicing the dragon dance, Anh and I decided it would be a good time to eat the rice cakes. We found an empty bench in a hallway and balanced the tray between us. We had the whole pile, yet we still chose our cakes carefully. Noi always took care to shape all of her portions into equal sizes, if for no other reason than to minimize squabbling. But we always felt that some pieces were bigger than others, or heavier, indicating more pork and rice within. Anh took a large bite right away, but I liked to take my time, finding more pleasure in the unwrapping. I liked that first glimpse of green, glossy rice, the leaf color soaked right through it. The musty, Saigon Market smell of the bean paste filled my nose as I bit into the cake. For a while we sat there, happily chewing away. The day was shaping up to be a good one—money, more food at home, excused from class, and an entire tray of treats to ourselves. It was like Baldwin Street all over again, just my sister and me hanging on to precious bundles of saved food.

Then Mrs. Hanley walked by and stopped short. "Oh, girls," she said. "These are for everyone." And just like that, she took the *banh chung* away from us. We knew then that they would be going to the Land of Sharing, of white people looking and declining. The cakes would grow crusty and stale under the recoiling gazes of our classmates. They would be ruined by the staring.

At the assembly, after the usual Pledge of Allegiance (me murmuring "one nation, under Buddha, for witches' stands"), a surprise song burst from the speakers: Neil Diamond singing, *On the boats and on the planes, they're coming to America! Never looking back again, they're coming to America!* My stepmother, who loved Neil Diamond, often sang this at home, calling out, "This song is about you! It's about boat people! You're a refugee, honey!" while she swayed to the thundering drumbeats. I was mortified that someone had created such a song and I wanted him to shut up. I especially hated the way he drew out the word *Today!*, his voice growing softer with each repeat. Sitting with the other Vietnamese kids in the school gym, I stared down at my feet—my brown loafers looked so clumsy and ugly with my *ao dai*—and wished the record player would explode.

Finally the music subsided and I could look up to concentrate on the dragon song. A group of boys set the long dragon costume over their heads and began rollicking across the gym floor. The other students sat cross-legged around the perimeter, watching the dragon's face shining with flecks of gold and green, red tassels flying. Its huge eyes and wide, grinning smile had an almost sinister look. The dragon circled the gym to the tune of the dragon song, loud with cymbals and bass, playing on a boom box that sat on the stage with the principal and several of the teachers. In spite of my discomfort, I loved the spectacle of the dragon, the fear and joy in its face, the way its head cocked to and fro in time to the beats. Someone had decorated the wall behind them with little paper roosters and the words "*Chuc mung nam moi*—Happy New Year" in yellow letters cut out of construction paper.

When the show was over, Mr. Ho called up all of us Vietnamese kids to the stage. This was a surprise, but I followed directions, lining up with Anh and Loan in a timid row while the white kids stared at us from the court lines. Mr. Ho made some speech about the Vietnamese people and thanked everyone at Chamberlain for being so welcoming. Miss Huong appeared then with a bundle of red roses in her arms. She faced us kids and beckoned right at me. I didn't move until Anh gave me a sharp nudge. Then I stumbled forward, and Miss Huong handed me the roses, telling me to give them to Mrs. Bailey, the principal. As I did so, feeling like a first-grade, first-class idiot, Rosa snapped a picture from somewhere in the back of the gymnasium. Later, Anh and I helped pass out Botan rice candies while our classmates milled around peeking at the *cha gio* that some of the parents had set up on tables. I saw our piles of green sticky rice cakes there, uneaten, and did not dare take another.

That weekend I put on the red *ao dai* again and danced at the Marriott Hotel while a group of mostly Vietnamese watched us with soft, misty-eyed faces. Loan and I had gotten into an argument the day before—something about who was a better dancer and who had the nicer *ao dai*. At the Marriott we met each other with cold eyes. We went around each other with our precise steps, tapping the drums at even intervals. As the high-pitched voice of the singer blared from the speakers, singing something about the beautiful arrival of spring, we danced and swayed and stepped as we had been taught, more or less in unison. Loan and I glared at each other as we pivoted, faced each other, and pivoted again. "Shut up," she muttered as she swept past me. "You shut up," I replied.

But as soon as the dance ended and people burst into applause, we couldn't help smiling. We looked at each other. We were nearly the same, two Vietnamese girls, friends and dance partners. At the reception, we made up over plates of *cha gio*, doughy dumplings stuffed with Chinese sausage, and *gio lua*, a peppery, bologna-like meat that resembled, in color and texture, the back of an old man's hard-worked hand. We could have been twins, we decided. We liked all the same foods. We talked about pizza and hamburgers and ice cream. We both liked Blue Moon flavor, as well as Superman, orange sherbet, and mint chocolate chip.

We were the best of friends all that year and the next, when I no longer had Anh to accompany me to school. Rosa had transferred her to Ken-O-Sha Elementary, three blocks from our house, where I would be going, too, the following year. Until then, I enjoyed the cold, solitary mornings waiting on the corner for the bus to Chamberlain. I took to singing as loud as I could, trying to fill up the sky, shouting out the words to Peter, Paul & Mary's "Leaving on a Jet Plane," Air Supply's "Here I Am," and "Harden My Heart" by Quarterflash.

At school, Loan and I spent every recess together. Once, she invited me to go home with her. The bus ride was a lot longer than mine, wending halfway to downtown Grand Rapids. They lived in a drafty house with a tilted front porch that reminded me of the house on Baldwin Street. In the living room, someone had propped up a big picture of a crackling fire in front of the fireplace. Loan and I played board games with little enthusiasm; the house felt chilly and dim, and Loan's parents were tense and angry about something. Her mother slammed the oven shut as she prepared a dinner of Jeno's frozen pizza. It was such a small pizza and I didn't understand how it would feed Loan, her parents, and her brother. When they offered me a slice I said no. I said my father was going to pick me up any minute. I sat in the living room and waited, the smell of the sausage crumbles making my stomach growl. From the couch I could see how hunched Loan's father looked as he sat at the kitchen table.

Around this time, in 1982, the Vietnamese parties seemed to begin in earnest, or perhaps I just became more aware of them. There were well over four thousand refugees in the Grand Rapids area, most of them clustered in southside suburbs like Kentwood and Wyoming. Many of the men worked in factories, no matter what their training had been in Vietnam; my father, I learned years later, had once apprenticed with an optometrist in Saigon. While a number of Vietnamese were Catholic, most of the families we knew were Buddhist, and the first time I saw the familiar statue and pile of fruit in someone else's house I felt a rush of solidarity. It was a feeling that would grow complicated as I grew older, a feeling that I would want to tuck away for myself, for this separate Vietnamese world.

Back then, driving out to one of the parties felt like a production, though we only lived ten or fifteen minutes away from where most of the other Vietnamese people lived. Everyone went except Crissy, who always insisted on staying home, and all of us fussed with our clothing, even Noi. It was a little daunting to go to Thanh Saigon Market's huge house in a fancy subdivision, named for a rolling crest or hill. His soaring white-walled rooms were filled with leather furniture, bold brass light fixtures, and mahogany tables inlaid with mother-of-pearl. But soon Noi joined the women crowded in the kitchen, gossiping while they fried *cha gio* and *banh xeo* crepes. In the dining room, the men welcomed my father and poured fresh bottles of cognac, alternating them with cans of Budweiser while they played cards. If they ever needed something they would just shout toward the stairway to the basement, where the kids played Atari, Hungry Hungry Hippo, and ping-pong; like all good Vietnamese kids, we would drop any activity to do an adult's bidding. Woven between our games, we traded knowledge of TV and music. We eyed each other's clothes. We all watched *Sesame Street* and *The Electric Company*. We were all obsessed with *Silver Spoons, Solid Gold,* and music videos. My sisters and I had watched the beginning of MTV the previous year, after our uncles had ordered cable for their setup downstairs and my father had spliced the wire up to the living room. We especially loved Blondie's soft-lit "Rapture" and how the Go-Go's promised "Our Lips Are Sealed."

Loan and her family almost never came to these parties, and I learned later that her father, who had opened his own grocery, had a rivalry with Thanh. The next year, when I transferred to Ken-O-Sha in time for third grade, Loan and I lost touch altogether. I took up with Marybelle, a new Vietnamese friend I had met at the Vietnamese parties. Named for the woman who had sponsored her family, Marybelle had a fierce-faced father who owned both a red Fiero and a bronze Firebird; her pretty, model-thin mother worked in alterations at Roger's Department Store. But I never stopped wondering about Loan. I remembered how unhappy and grim her family had seemed, and the memory prevented me from calling her at home. I wondered what she did on Saturday nights instead of coming to the parties.

Rosa was nearly as left out, with no clear purpose there, and no one to talk to. As soon as the men settled down with cards she knew she was on her own. I saw her once, as I came upstairs for more shrimp chips, standing at the edge of the kitchen doorway, watching my father play poker. He was losing, as he always did when he drank too much. Rosa had a look on her face that I only saw sometimes when she was around my father—part timid, part passive. It was the same look she had when she asked him what she should wear to an event. It was unsettling to me—it was not the stepmother I knew. She would not have dared to interrupt the poker game and demand we go home any more than I would have.

❧

We went on like this for a couple of years until suddenly, we didn't. Maybe it was Anh wanting to stay home to talk on the phone with friends and boys and me wanting to copy her. Maybe it was the increasing tension of the parties themselves, Rosa's growing disapproval and my father's irritation at the disapproval. Noi had shifted her social life to her Buddhist temple gatherings on Sundays, and gradually there seemed to be no good reason to go to parties anymore. So my father went alone. I rather enjoyed his absence, the way it felt a little easier to breathe when he was away. I never realized how much on edge I felt—perhaps we all felt—when he was at home, usually moody, prone to a fit of yelling if someone so much as changed the volume of the stereo. I got the feeling that the person he was at the parties was the person he preferred to be—young, as he had been in Vietnam, surrounded by laughter and friends, drinking and smoking away his troubles.

At home I watched TV, slowly eating a pudding snack to try to make it last through as much as possible of the NBC Saturday night lineup, which included, at various times, *Gimme a Break!*, *Diff'rent Strokes*, *The Facts of Life*, *The Golden Girls*, and *227*. Or I played our Intellivision video games—Lock 'n' Chase (a poor man's Pac-Man), skiing, and poker. I spent hours honing my blackjack skills, facing the crudely pixellated dealer who laughed evilly when the house won. I coaxed Anh to play Rubik's Race with me, or Monopoly or Life. If I was super bored I played with the doll heads that someone had given us, so we could practice cosmetology and hairdressing. The dolls were life-sized busts, with plastic faces and thick heads of sandy blond hair, and they came with palettes of makeup and brushes. Anh could give her doll curls, pinned-up French braids, complicated eye shadows, and inventive lipstick tints. My doll always ended up looking the same. Eventually I would retreat to my books, eavesdropping on my sisters' phone conversations. The house would feel dim and closed-down. Rosa would be working at the dining room table and all of us would go to bed long before my father came home.

In the fall of 1986, when I was twelve years old, my father got the idea to throw a dance hall party. A fabulous one that would draw people from all over, that would have everyone talking for weeks. He'd taken Rosa to a few such parties at rented VFW halls or the Ramada Inn, where DJs mixed ballroom tunes with Barbra Streisand ballads. A band might play, led by mellow-voiced Vietnamese singers crooning beneath a disco ball. These were cover-charge, cash-bar parties, with big dance floors where my father could show off his smooth moves, spinning Rosa around while other couples just watched. For that was his ace in the hole, the one thing that could always soften Rosa into a smile. The Vietnamese Arthur Murray, she sometimes called him, then she'd shake her hips, saying, "Cha-cha-cha!"

Together with a friend he rented out a dance hall and managed to book a semi-famous Vietnamese lady singer who agreed to travel from Chicago to Grand Rapids for the event. The cover charge and cash bar would, my father planned, net a tidy profit. I was nervous about the party—nothing would be worse than a low attendance—and about the task my father had given me and Anh:

to go around picking up the empty cans of pop and beer so we could return them later for the ten-cent deposits.

It had been nearly two years since the last Vietnamese party I'd attended and I felt like a stranger; I hated my big new braces and weird hair that never would feather properly the way Anh's did. And I recognized almost none of the people who were arriving except Marybelle, the only Vietnamese kid I really knew besides my sister and the one other Vietnamese girl in my class at school.

We staked out a spot in the back to check out the women in their shiniest *ao dais* and men in their dark suits. Some of the younger women had exchanged traditional dress for American outfits—satin cocktail dresses, panty hose, and high-heeled pumps. They gathered at the round tables and started drinking. They threw back their heads to blow cigarette smoke into the air, and laughed raucously at nothing. All night, Anh and I maneuvered around them with our plastic trash bags, gingerly collecting empty cans of Budweiser. The semi-famous singer wouldn't arrive until later, so everyone danced to the DJ's moody Vietnamese rhumba and tango songs. People paused to watch my father. He moved with such ease, a sense of gliding. He whirled Rosa around, passing other couples without ever grazing them. He danced as if they were alone on the floor. Women lined up to take a turn with him, which seemed to make Rosa both jealous and proud.

To please the younger crowd, my father had hired a local group of Vietnamese guys to be the opening act for the lady singer. The guys of Y White, in their late teens and early twenties, rode the new wave with their billowy black pants, white collared shirts buttoned to the neck, and spiky gelled hair—buzzed

in the back, mop-floppy in front. Y White played covers of Era-
sure, New Order, and Depeche Mode. My favorite was their ren-
dition of "Oh L'amour." As the slow opening notes gave way to
drums someone in the band flicked on a strobe light. Then all the
guys began dancing, their white shirts glowing as their arms flailed
in staccato motions. All the kids got on the dance floor then and
I watched, straining to remember who they were. I thought I saw
Thanh Saigon Market's pretty daughter until she blended into
the crowd.

After Y White finished their set, word went around that the
lady singer had finally arrived with her entourage. She floated
onto the stage in a sequined red *ao dai*, looking like one of the
graceful ladies on the scroll calendars from the Saigon Market:
super sleek hair swinging around their waists; impossibly smooth
faces heavy with makeup; bodies reed-thin, clad always in bright
silk. When the semi-famous lady singer sang, her mouth curved
into a pretty oval shape and her head tilted just so to convey the
melancholy of the music. She sang operatically, sorrowfully, but
with a glint in her eye. She was as flawless and unreal as a heroine
in a soap opera, and the spotlight never strayed from her. When
she lifted her arm in time to a high-pitched note her dress threw
out sparks of light. The crowd cheered and clapped. It was the
one great moment of my father's brief career as a party maker.

From a table at the back I tried to catch the lady singer's
notes, to understand what she was saying. I couldn't. The drawn-
out syllables soared toward the rotating disco ball and out of my
reach. I felt alone, distant from the other Vietnamese kids who
had formed an intimidating group at their own table. I tried to
picture what my friends from school were doing at that instant.
Probably Holly Jansen was asleep, her face like porcelain in the

moonlight. Holly's mother would have tucked her into bed, which I imagined involved pulling the covers tight to strap her in. I could never explain to her, or to any of my friends from school, what happened at Vietnamese parties. They would have been scandalized by the alcohol, the late hours. To them the Vietnamese lady singer would have seemed funny-sounding—abnormal rather than beautiful. She didn't belong in my friends' world, I told myself. She only made sense here, in this hidden-away place, this undercover club with its coded foreign language.

Later, after the lady singer had departed in a cloud of admiration, after all the guests had drifted off, my father and his friend sat at a table and counted the cash. My sister and I walked around collecting the last cans. My uncles had taken Noi and Vinh home a while ago, but Anh and I had to stay to help with cleanup. Crissy never came to these kinds of parties, and no one ever made her. I figured she was fast asleep at home—it was past two in the morning by the time the party wrapped up—and I envied that. I envied the ease with which she could say, *No, I won't go,* and have it be final. She had a choice. She could pass as normal and I could not.

My father spent a long time counting and recounting the night's earnings. I heard him trade words with his friend, his voice rising in anger. As we drove home in silence it was clear that the party had been a financial bust. The cost of hiring the lady singer had been so high that in spite of the good turnout he hadn't broken even. After that night my father no longer talked about making money by throwing parties or opening a club. He retreated. At home he did woodwork in the garage, weeded the garden, or fiddled with the car engine. At night he played pool at Anazeh Sands or poker at his friends' houses.

The dance party had left me with a vague feeling of loss I couldn't shake. It magnified at school, when Holly might ask what I did over the weekend and I would say, *nothing*. I told myself there was no point in socializing with the other Vietnamese kids, who went to different schools and whose parents knew each other better. The parties always went on too long anyway, ending with us kids falling asleep and pissing off our parents by clamoring to go home. Surely I could find contentment in my familiar books, markers, and construction paper while Anh hung out with her friends. That was the kind of social life I needed to cultivate: weekend afternoons at Holly's house or Tammy's house or Mindy's house. School-sponsored Saturdays at the Woodland Skating Rink, where I, gawky with my glasses and braces, never once skated during "couples only," when the DJ played songs like Billy Ocean's "Suddenly" and REO Speedwagon's "In My Dreams." I liked the darkness of the rink and even though I could never skate very well or fast, I cherished the freedom of movement, of trying to fly beyond people's range of vision.

One of the last Vietnamese events I remember attending happened a few months after the dance hall party. It was right after Tet, which had fallen on a school day. Though we'd had permission to stay home for the holiday, all of us kids had gone to school. We had recently moved to Ada, a suburb of Grand Rapids, and Tet had felt worn-down, fractured; some unnamed tension disturbed the joy of red envelopes, *cha gio,* and bean cakes. But that weekend, perhaps out of restlessness, Anh and I went along with our father and Noi to a party in southeast Grand Rapids. I remember I wore a mustard-colored shirt, handed down from Crissy, that still maintained an aura of her coolness, and Anh fretted over her curling-iron curls. At the party our father and Noi joined their own friends and Anh and I stood together, feeling out of place. The fact was clear: the other Vietnamese kids had been united all that time we had stayed at home. They had shared holidays and birthdays and board games. They knew each other, had grown up together, and had no need for us. They sat in a group, laughing and speaking a flurry of mixed Vietnamese and English. And at the center of them all was the daughter of Thanh Saigon Market, Tiffany née Truoc. She had grown taller, more willowy, and more beautiful than ever. She was almost tall enough not to be considered "so short," which is the comment Anh and I were used to getting at school—"You're so short!" followed by some tall person trying to use our head as an armrest. Tiffany-Truoc also had the benefit of a wealthy father, and thus a Swatch watch, Forenza sweater, and stone-washed Guess jeans. She flaunted them as she flaunted her own curtain of hair, shiny as a Vietnamese lady singer's. Seeing Tiffany hold court, I realized that Anh and I had missed out on an entire system, a structure, what Rosa called *community*.

"Let's just eat," Anh murmured as we approached the long buffet tables. I thought of previous holiday parties, when we could choose from half a dozen different kinds of *cha gio* or *banh chung*, all cooked by different women who watched anxiously to see whose would be eaten first. Every time, no one's dishes could compare to Noi's. The other *cha gio* were all wrong—too thin or too thick, rolled too loosely, too much noodle, not enough shrimp, too pasty, too bland, too soggy. I once saw a woman in a canary-yellow *ao dai* repeatedly check on the trays she had brought: still there. Meanwhile, Noi's *cha gio,* stacked in golden pyramids, disappeared. She had brought them again this time, the wrinkle and fry of them as familiar to me as my books. I heaped several on a plate, moving on to pickled vegetables, noodles, shrimp chips, and puff pastry shells stuffed with ground pork. Anh headed straight for the doughy balls stuffed with Chinese sausage and the square cakes of *banh chung* tied with string. We sat down in a corner of the living room, just the two of us.

Instead of digging in I looked at three girls approaching the buffet. They seemed to be about my age, and they were making jokes to each other I couldn't understand. Their talking made my cheeks burn. Why hadn't I practiced my Vietnamese? Why hadn't I kept up? Each day I struggled to remember even simple words to communicate with Noi; now all I had were her *cha gio*. I worried that the girls at the buffet were snickering at me and Anh and calling us Twinkies—yellow on the outside, white on the inside. Was that what I had longed to achieve, after all? I remembered the defiant guys of Y White, their name a statement instead of a question. A demand. I wondered what had happened to them, if they were singing their own songs now or if they had broken up and drifted away.

Sitting next to me, Anh was unwrapping a *banh chung* cake, peeling the banana leaf away to unveil the familiar mass of glutinous rice the color of pale jade. She lifted it to her mouth and bit off a corner. As she chewed she held out the cake to me, raising her eyebrows to ask if I wanted a bite. I said okay. The heft of it surprised me, as always, as I grasped the cake between my fingers. I leaned in to smell the mung bean paste, which reminded me of dark, still moments in Noi's bedroom just after her evening meditation. It occurred to me then that I was in a place that none of my friends from school would ever understand or even know. It occurred to me that I had always had choices: to go to parties or not. To call my friend Loan or not. To keep up my Vietnamese or not. To tell my friends at school, *My father threw a party once and hired a lady singer and a band called Y White.* I bit into the rice cake, its sticky sweetness scenting my tongue. It tasted like a secret long kept, old and familiar and unspeakable.

9

Down with Grapes

THE WORLD IS FULL OF MOTHERS.

Jennifer's mother played the piano and made chocolate chip cookies and Kool-Aid pops.

Holly's mother baked Jiffy muffins and packed pizza lunches and thermoses of Campbell's chicken noodle soup.

The imperfect mothers, like Mrs. Harrison next door, worked all the time. We hardly ever saw her, but knew that the other mothers gossiped about how she had married and divorced a black man. The kids, Janie and Linc, mostly kept to themselves. With their brown skin and deaf cat, they were as freakish as we were. We liked the Harrisons because they didn't care about their lawn, either, and didn't care if we played in their backyard in the winter, stepping onto their property just to see our footprints in new snow.

Down the street, Kim and Becky Doornbos's mother stayed inside all day long. Kim had long blond hair like Marcia Brady and Becky was strawberry blond. Becky was the bratty sister, while Kim spoke in whispers. They weren't allowed to leave the vicinity of their property and only desperate boredom led Anh and me to play with them. There was something eerie about the Doornbos girls. They were odder-looking than we were, which was saying something. One time, Becky got stuck on the swing set rings, her thick knees refusing to slip out, and she hung there upside down, screaming and smiling at the same time. Kim just gazed at her. Mrs. Doornbos came running out, her hair still in pink curlers. "Kim, you dummy," she rasped. "Help her out!"

Then there was Tara's mother, who introduced me to beef Stroganoff and showed me that I had no manners.

Tara was Anh's friend from school, but when she invited Anh to spend a day at her house during holiday break, Rosa insisted that I had to be invited as well. I was seven years old then and still followed my sister everywhere. That early afternoon Tara and her mother picked us up in their blue Cherokee. They had matching honey-brown bob haircuts and down jackets. Their car had no dog smells, no Burger King wrappers on the floor, no sticky cans of 7UP rolling around in the back. As we drove to Studio 28 to see a showing of the *Cinderella* movie, Tara and her mother sang along to a tape of Disney songs. At the theater, Tara's mother bought us pop, bags of popcorn, and M&M's. The generosity shamed me. On the rare occasion that my parents took us to a movie they smuggled candy and cans of RC and Vernors in Rosa's massive purse.

After Cinderella had been whisked away in the Prince's chariot we went to Tara's house, which rose up in a tower of blushing brick and white shutters. In the entryway a staircase curved into a balcony, and glossy hardwood floors led to the Christmas tree still lit up in their living room. The opened gifts were arranged under the tree: a spiffy new pair of boots, a doll propped up against ornaments.

Tara was an only child, and her bedroom was a fantasy explosion of stuffed animals and the color pink. She had the canopy bed I had dreamed about, with lacy hems dripping over the edges. She had a huge dollhouse, each room fitted up with colonial furnishings and wallpaper, with decorative pillows on the bed and portraits on the walls. Tara and Anh banished me to the hallway bookshelf so they could play house by themselves and listen to the radio.

While I sifted through Tara's fairy-tale books the sky outside the window seeped into dusk. A meaty smell floated up the stairs, and I had a sudden panicky feeling of being a stowaway, of being caught. But then Tara's mother called us all down to dinner. My sister and I traded nervous looks. We had never had dinner at a house like this, so fine with its real Christmas tree and white upholstered furniture, nothing sullied by dog hair or spills of Sunny Maid. Anh and I lingered at the entrance of the formal dining room, awed by the chandelier we later agreed must have been made of diamonds.

At home we sat wherever we could at the table, pushing old copies of the *Grand Rapids Press* out of the way, taking care only to avoid the spot reserved for our ancestors, whose spirits my grandmother fed three times a day. At Tara's house there were no hungry spirits to worry about, and certainly no clutter, so I slipped into the first chair I saw.

That's when Tara's father came into the room and stopped short when he saw me sitting at the head of the table. He said nothing, nor did Tara's mother a moment later when she brought out the dinner plates. Only her flat stare told me I had done something wrong. I hadn't yet learned the rules about fathers and mothers, head and foot, the king and his castle.

I concentrated on the food before me: egg noodles sinking in brown gravy, buoys of beef and canned mushroom. It looked just like the commercials for Noodle Roni and I picked up my fork and started eating. Tara's mother set a basket of rolls on the table and cleared her throat. She had had enough. "In this house," she said, looking at me, "we pray before we eat."

I wanted then, as I did countless times after, for years, to slide away and vanish, become as unseeable as my ancestors. The humiliation burned through, bad enough for me to confess it to my stepmother later at home.

"Sounds like beef Stroganoff," she said.

I repeated the words to myself. "Is that fancy?"

"Well, it's not what poor people get to eat."

Then Rosa laughed at the idea of me sitting at the head of the table. "Don't you know you're not supposed to sit there? Don't you know you're supposed to wait until other people start eating?"

"Why didn't you tell me?" I demanded, but she just told me to be quiet now. I wanted to say: *Isn't it a mother's job to teach lessons on good manners? How am I supposed to know how to be a decent girl unless my mother shows me?* But Rosa was already moving, gathering her files for work, picking up the phone to make a call. She was way too busy, she said, to worry about things like that.

The lessons she preferred were more about hunger than manners. "Do you know how many children are starving in Africa?" she'd ask when one of us kids wouldn't finish a meal. "Think of the starving refugee children. *You* were a refugee," she'd add pointedly.

A few years later, just as I was about to enter fifth grade, the public school teachers went on strike. To show her support, Rosa refused to let any of us kids go to school until the teachers had returned. I called my best friend Holly, who confirmed that everyone had shown up on the first day except for me.

"Who's going to teach them?" I asked Rosa.

"Scabs," she hissed.

I pictured dry purplish scabs, like the ones that formed over my skinned knees, pacing in front of a chalkboard.

Anh and Crissy were thrilled about missing school, and Vinh seemed glad enough to stay at home with his Transformers and *He-Man* reruns, but I felt uneasy: the first days were foundational; friendships for the whole year could be cemented. I told Rosa that I needed to get back to school, but she said no way, José. "No one in our house is going to cross the picket lines."

Rosa loved a good strike. Her great hero was César Chávez, whom I learned about when she announced that we were all boycotting lettuce, grapes, and everything made by Campbell's. She wore buttons on her blazers: "Lettuce Stick Together" and "Down with Grapes." Campbell's and grapes: those were her enemies, and for a long time not a single grape appeared in our household, unless smuggled in by our uncles and grandmother. Rosa spoke of the fruit—picked in California by underpaid and exploited migrants—with such resentment that for years, even after the migrants had won a bit of victory and Rosa stopped boycotting, I still looked at grapes with apprehension. César Chávez had organized the migrant workers in California, a move that must have taken Rosa straight back to her own childhood, when her parents' wages depended on the seasons and the sums doled out by farms and orchards up and down the coast of Lake Michigan.

Rosa explained how the workers had no say and no power, and that only unions ensured that they would be paid fairly.

César Chávez appealed to my sense of justice, stirred from reading *The Grapes of Wrath*. It was one of my favorite books for its descriptions of dust, greasy food, and soulful characters. The biscuits were "high" and "bulbous"; Ma Joad "[lifted]…curling slices of pork from the frying pan." I found myself charmed by Tom Joad, a good man in spite of the years he'd done in prison. I felt his hunger when he came back from a day of picking peaches and shouted, "Leave me at her," while reaching for his dinner plate. The way he wolfed down his three hamburger patties and white bread with drippings drizzled on top. "Got any more?" he asked Ma. She kept the whole family going, but she didn't have any more food for Tom that night, not when wages were so little and store prices so high. They had seen families making their way eastward, back out of California, to go home to die in the dust they had tried to escape.

So my heart beat a little faster when Rosa decided to take Vinh and me to the picket line in front of Fountain Street Elementary School in downtown Grand Rapids. Against the backdrop of the old brick school and a sky-blue day, a small group of women clustered about the sidewalk, holding up signs. "Who are they?" I asked Rosa.

"Who do you think they are? The picketers, of course."

They carried plain signs—"FAIR WAGES! SUPPORT YOUR TEACHERS!"—as they walked back and forth, looking nothing like Tom Joad or Casey or Ma or Rosasharn. Things only got exciting when parents drove by, at which point the teachers started jumping and waving their signs. If they saw a scab they screamed, "Scab!" No one paid them any attention. No paid-off cops came to arrest them.

Vinh and I marched alongside Rosa and the other women for a while. It was early September and hot out, and we soon lamented not having any candy to keep us going. Other teachers showed up with thermoses of coffee, talking in serious tones about the lack of response from the superintendent. They looked indignant, and I rallied myself to feel the outrage I had felt when cops tried to arrest Tom's friend for "agitating," and when Casey got hit with the pick handle. I thought about how big corporations kept lowering wages, knowing that there were people waiting, and hungry enough, to take any worker's place. I tried to imagine Ma Joad among these teachers, walking heavily in her faded calico print dress.

The teachers ended the strike two weeks later with only some of their demands met. I started school mostly worried that my classmates were already sailing far ahead of me. Cliques might have been formed, desks decorated and arranged. I would be the odd one out, the one anxious to find a seat in the cafeteria, the one having to court all over again the blue-eyed girls who held the keys to popularity.

As it happened, Holly said the scabs had been like substitute teachers. They'd spent the days reading and drawing and going over last year's easy math. I hadn't missed much at all. At recess on my first day back I felt so comfortable that I bragged that I had joined the picket line, until Jamie Taylor, who always dressed up as a princess for Halloween and whose mother had once sent her to school with a platter of homemade rosette cookies dusted with powdered sugar, called me a Communist. When I denied it she shrugged and said, "Your *mom's* a Communist."

"She is not," I said, thinking of how Rosa spoke of Communists with foreboding in her voice, and how she warned me that if they "took over" we would have no more liberties.

Jamie Taylor pointed out, "You're the only one whose mom didn't let her come to school during the strike."

Her words reinforced the shame I already felt: I did not have a mother who stayed home to clean the bathrooms and bake angel food cakes. Rosa worked downtown, near the "bad" part of the city, directing GED and ESL classes at the Hispanic Institute. She liked to bring us kids there on weekends and after school, to help run the mimeograph machine and tidy up the classrooms. The building had been an elementary school in the sixties and now it seemed to soak up dust on every surface. Grime coated the windows and gritted the vinyl floors. Inside the main hall, someone had painted a fantastic mural in the style of Diego Rivera. A bald eagle and a brown-faced man faced each other, and around them groups of American Indians, African-Americans, and Latino-Americans looked on, wearing proud, impassioned expressions. Above them a banner unscrolled the words "We the People of America" and *Viva la raza!* The vending machines stood near the mural, so I spent a lot of time staring at it. I felt the bold eyes watching me; the colors—all browns and russets streaked with red—followed me down the hall as I wandered in and out of classrooms, looking for something to read, teaching myself the Spanish words for the months and days. I scanned bilingual education phrase books. We had some at home, including one devoted to explanations of American idioms like "go jump in a lake" or "get out of town." My father always got these wrong. When he didn't know the answer to something he'd shrug and say, "Beat me."

The previous year Rosa had enrolled me in an evening cake-decorating class. While she caught up on paperwork in her office, I and a half dozen middle-aged Mexican-American women learned how to mix buttercream frosting and use silver nozzles fastened onto pastry bags to create stars, letters, and flowers. For my final project I decorated a cake with a pink unicorn prancing in a field of violets. I enjoyed the class—the murmur of the ladies fretting over their scalloped borders, the swirl of dye into frosting, the effort involved in each sugar rose. But it frustrated me that I could never frost a cake in even waves the way the women on commercials and in the Sunday coupons did. Their round two-layer confections, lavishly coated in Betty Crocker whipped frostings, never sloped or showed crumbs. I became convinced that such talents lay only in the hands of white mothers in aprons. To me, life lived in commercials *was* real life. Commercials were instructions; they were news. They showed me what perfection could be: in the right woman's hands, the layers of a cake would always be exactly the same size. In the right woman's kitchen, a cartoon rabbit would visit the children and show them how to slurp down a tall glass of Nestlé Quik with a straw. A shaken cruet would spill a stream of Good Seasons over hills of lettuce leaves. Commercials had a firm definition of motherhood, which almost all of my friends' mothers had no trouble fulfilling. They swept floors and scrubbed bathtubs. They cooked casseroles and washed dishes. They had smooth, sensible pageboy hairstyles and serene smiles. They set the dinner tables every night and sang Cinderella songs and taught their children where to sit.

My siblings and I were always plaguing Rosa to buy things we saw on TV. Instead of the generic raisin bran and Toasty-O's, which came in big bags that were slung onto the bottom shelf of the cereal aisle, we campaigned for Trix, Cookie Crisp, Franken Berry, and Count Chocula. We begged for any kind that came with buried trinkets—stickers, spokes, tattoo stamps. We created our own ads for orange juice, reenacted the commercials for Life cereal (Vinh always played Mikey), and sang the Carnation Instant Breakfast song: "You're gonna love it in an instant!"

On rare weekends, Rosa or Crissy made pancakes or French toast with blueberries we had picked and frozen the previous summer. That's when the trusty bottle of Mrs. Butterworth's syrup came out. I loved that her body was the bottle, which seemed both perverse and alluring. In the commercials, when kids talked to her she came to life, her arms gesturing regally as she spoke. I waited for her to speak to me, too, staring at her placid face to will her to life. Sometimes, too, I shouted "Hey, Kool-Aid!" but the giant pitcher of Mr. Kool-Aid never did come crashing through a wall of our house.

Most of all, I would have given so much to have the Pillsbury Doughboy appear in our kitchen. He would bounce across the counter like a living marshmallow and wave his wee rolling pin at me. His puffy white chef's hat would almost fall off and he would spread his arms to welcome me to his world. Then, at last, I would reach out and poke his belly with the tip of my finger, making him coo and giggle, his round eyes scrunching up with laughter.

All of my stepmother's talk about boycotts and Chávez had given me the brilliant idea of going on strike at dinnertime. It started one night when she made another big pan of Mexican rice strewn with stewed tomatoes and pieces of boiled chicken thighs. I said I was sick and tired of eating the same things—*pho* and stir-fries, *sopa* and rice—and I was going on strike until we started eating better food.

"There are migrant children starving right now," Rosa told me. "Think of all the girls your age in Vietnam who are starving. You could have been one of them. If the Communists came here right now do you know what would happen?"

"I don't care," I shouted, suddenly determined. Let the Communists come.

By this time it was just the two of us at the table. My father was off somewhere with his friends, as he was all the time now, playing pool at Anazeh Sands, convinced he could bring home profits from gambling. Rosa said I was lucky he wasn't home. "You're cruisin' for a bruisin'," she said, one of her favorite phrases. She announced that I would be staying at the table until I finished my plate of rice.

My temper boiled up. "You can't tell me what to do." The words tumbled out. "You're not my real mother." It was the first time I ever acknowledged it.

You're a scab, I almost said, but a piercing fear held me back.

Rosa glared at me, shocked, and walked away. I sat in my chair for a while, waiting for punishment, but nothing happened. Finally I got up and slinked off to my grandmother's room.

For the next couple of days Rosa didn't look at me at all. Then the weekend arrived, and she woke everyone up with the sound of the vacuum running at seven in the morning, something that had never happened before in our house. She barged into the room I shared with Crissy and Anh and threw our clothes out of her way as she bore the vacuum over the green carpet. She started cleaning everything. She dusted and mopped and scrubbed tiles in the bathroom, all the while her face set in a grim mask. My siblings and I tiptoed around her, afraid to speak or interrupt. Noi, sensing trouble, stayed in her room. At lunchtime Rosa slapped down paper plates heaped with Kraft macaroni and cheese and chicken nuggets. That's when she finally spoke. "Eat it all," she barked. "This is what you want to eat, well, you'd better eat it."

But the tension had drained our appetites, and when she went off to clean the bathroom we threw the food away, forgetting to think about the girls and boys starving in Communist countries. Anh and Crissy, pissed at me for starting all the trouble, refused to talk to me, so Vinh and I holed up in the basement to play Chinese checkers. My father seemed never to come home. For dinner Rosa dished up large portions of my coveted Noodle Roni. But none of us ate much, and without a word she picked up our plates and heaved them into the trash.

This went on for two more days, Rosa serving foods my sisters and I had always clamored to have: Chef Boyardee, frozen pizza, scalloped potatoes from a box. But we could not enjoy it. My sisters glowered and Rosa spoke to no one. The food itself began to feel heavy, slicked with the artificial flavorings and colorings promised right on the packages. I didn't know how much more I could take of such silence and abundance.

Then, as abruptly as she had started, Rosa stopped. One day Noi was back in the kitchen heating up her seafood soup; the cloud over the house had lifted. My stepmother and I never spoke of our standoff, for she had sent her message. This was what it would be like if she, like all of my friends' mothers, stayed at home. This was what it would be like never to have blissful solitude, to be watched and cleaned and fed and fed and fed. I never again wished for Rosa to be what Jennifer's mother proudly called herself: a homemaker.

No, this was the mother I had. Neither royal nor rich, nor yet a woman like Ma Joad, who had huddled with a dead body in the back of a jalopy just so her family could get across the desert. For a long time, the sting of the words I had thrown at Rosa stayed with me. She was not, in fact, my real mother, but I never said it again.

I could shed tears for the Joads, but I did not wish to imagine other Nguyens working for food in Vietnam. I knew the dragon shape of the country, its gauntness and curves, but I couldn't imagine where my actual mother could be in it: where she lived, what she did, what she thought about at night when she was alone. Or was she alone? I didn't know that, either. I had no photo to comprehend, no voice to recall, not even a description or a name. I pictured a random Vietnamese woman eating *pho* the way my father and uncles did—faces bent toward the steaming bowl to suck all the flavor in—but her face remained blank. She could have been any of the women who pushed past me in the tight aisles of the Saigon Market.

I had several worlds—the one inside the house, the one outside in Grand Rapids, and the one that existed in my books and diaries and on television. These were always colliding, and my real mother fit in none of them. Her existence, vague as it was, complicated all of the ones I had arranged so carefully for myself.

Better, then, to stay silent, too, keep our house unrippled by questions. What I didn't know was that all that time she had been making plans. While I studied fractions and followed once again the path of the Joads along Route 66, immigrants in their own country, my real mother was out there, too, threading her way to the United States.

Bread and Honey

MY STEPSISTER CRISSY WAS ALWAYS IN CHARGE. WHEN she decided that it would be neat to wear fluorescent pink with royal blue, I wanted to wear that, too. When she sang "Bette Davis Eyes," I learned the words, too. She determined what songs were cool, what clothes were cool, and whether or not we were cool. Invariably, I was not. She called me "Nerd," but that didn't stop me from aspiring to be in her realm. Crissy had always been fresh and pretty, with a fine smattering of freckles across her nose and dark hair that fell in natural waves. Her best friends were Keri and Lisa, girls knowledgeable about boys and nail polish; Lisa even owned a scandalous triangle bikini. Anh and I longed to be a part of their giggles and codes.

Crissy could talk Rosa into letting her stay up late to watch TV. She persuaded Rosa to buy her some Calvin Klein socks so Crissy could snip off the labels and sew them onto her clothes. When school-picture time rolled around she somehow managed to get Rosa to spring for more expensive backgrounds—the woodsy one with a fake piece of timber to cross her arms on, or the laser-light one that had zigzagging neon bars to impart a hint of *Miami Vice*. Crissy had reign over our bedroom, bathroom, and television. She could change the channel if she felt like it, right in the middle of my and Anh's beloved *Bugs Bunny/Road Runner* show. Later, she was the first in the neighborhood to tease her hair into airy claw shapes, highlighting it with peroxide and Sun-In; she rolled up the hems of her pants until they were tight and tapered. She would show up with lacy fingerless gloves, plastic bracelets, and purple shimmery lipstick, and I would wonder how she managed to get such beautiful things.

Those hazy, early eighties summers on Florence Street meld together in patches of shade and the sound of the ice cream man pushing through the neighborhood. It seemed like no parents were ever around. They simply let us kids loose as soon as we woke up and didn't see us until evening when we swept into the house, dusty and sweaty from a day of games. While Jennifer Vander Wal and I devised elaborate, exclusive clubs, Crissy and her friends rode their ten-speeds and played Capture the Black Flag.

One of Crissy's favorite things to do was explore the tangle of backyards and fences that made up the center of our neighborhood block of houses. Once, she allowed Anh and me to tag along while she and her friends trampled through people's gardens. We went right into their toolsheds if the doors were open. One shed, belonging to a neighbor no one knew, was locked and windowless, and Crissy said it might be haunted. Either that or the man kept dead bodies in there. We crept past it and circled the guy's house, always following Crissy.

At last, when she grew weary and hungry enough, she led us to someone's overgrown garden where rhubarb grew thickly among weeds. Crissy snapped some up and carried them back to our cement front stoop, where she pulled from her pocket a plastic bag of sugar. She licked a stalk of rhubarb to make it sticky, plunged it into the bag of sugar, and took a big bite. She passed the sugar and rhubarb around to Keri, Lisa, and finally Anh and me. By the time I got the bag it was damp with spittle; grains of sugar stuck to my hands. Up close, I saw that the stalk might have been celery, the green eclipsed by a scarlet hue that stained its way upward. In my experience, red things tasted good—red cherry Luden's cough drops, red Life Savers, red strawberries, but this rhubarb didn't look so promising. Still I ground it into the sugar and took a bite, startled when a bitter, sour taste filled my mouth. The sugar became grit between my teeth; the rhubarb broke into strands, refusing to dissolve. I stopped chewing, afraid Crissy would catch my reaction. But it was too late—she rolled her eyes. If the rhubarb was an admission test, I was failing it.

Then she jumped up and said, "Come on, guys, I wanna show you something," and led the way inside to the kitchen. I followed, too, gathering with the others at the counter, where Crissy set out a loaf of white bread and a jar of honey. She said, "Watch this." She closed her fist around a slice of bread, crushing it, collapsing its shape back into dough. Dimpled with her fingerprints, the bread looked like a ball of clay. She put it on a plate and doused it with streams of honey. "This is sooo good," she promised us. She stuck her fingers right into the ball of bread, honey and all, and sank her teeth into it.

Anh, Keri, and Lisa all molded their own bread balls and ate them with honey, while the slice that Crissy had given me remained in my hands. There was something repulsive, something gruesome, about breaking down the bread. I wanted it to stay firm and spongy, a pallet for cheese and meat, jelly and peanut butter. I couldn't bear the thought of destroying its shape. Crissy took in my frozen stance with another eye-roll. "You're such a wimp," she sighed.

Usually whatever she liked, the rest of us siblings liked. Canned mushrooms eaten straight from the can. Condensed cream of mushroom soup heated up with half the amount of water, to intensify the saltiness. Scrambled eggs with peas, eaten on a warmed-up tortilla. Avocados sliced and sprinkled with salt. French toast. Cheesecake. Anything with tomatoes. The only desserts Rosa made: warm chocolate pudding and flan, the thin caramel liquid spooned over the slippery custard. I was used to following Crissy's orders on what to eat, wear, watch on TV, or listen to. I believed in her knowledge of the world, but could not bring myself to eat what she offered that day.

It's such a small thing—a stalk of rhubarb, a ball of bread and honey. Yet it's stark in my mind as a moment of withholding. A moment of dissent, marking myself as the one who would not go along, into the club of girlhood.

During the summer that Rosa finished her master's degree in education at Grand Valley State, she sometimes took Anh, Crissy, and me along with her to campus. I must have been seven years old at the time. We would pull out of the driveway early in the morning, while Noi and Vinh stood at the living room window, waving good-bye. Vinh would be crying his eyes out, his red mouth wobbly with screams. The half-hour car trip to Allendale seemed endless, but Rosa talked up the greatness of college, where she said we would all go someday. The idea thrilled and intimidated us: a time when we would be pretty much grown-up, on our own. Walking across Grand Valley's campus filled me with awe—I, too, wanted to be one of the students striding past with such purpose, such determination in the gait.

On our first visit Rosa took us along paths that crisscrossed toward classroom buildings. All of the buildings looked like banks and insurance agencies. The prettiest spot on campus was a stone bridge over a narrow creek, lined with willow trees and plants I couldn't name. On each side of the bridge the banks of the creek sloped sharply. Rosa told us a story of a woman in a wheelchair who had pushed herself down the embankment to try to kill herself. I shivered at the conjured image—the back of a woman's head, her body bounding out of the careening chair and tumbling down the hill. But the woman had survived. What happened to her? I asked. Nobody knew.

Rosa did not want us wandering around campus while she was in class, and gave us strict instructions to stay inside the Student Union. She handed us each a couple of dollars to spend in the university bookstore and warned us not to leave the building. When Rosa went off to her classes, Crissy, Anh, and I went to the bookstore right away. I felt rich with my two dollars, and thought of all the candy I could buy. Four different kinds, I decided, at forty cents each, with a little left over to save. But once I saw that the bookstore had all kinds of notebooks, pads of paper, and pens, I reallotted the sum. After careful consideration I selected a blue-covered notepad, a red pen, and M&M's, for each individual piece could make the whole sack seem to last longer.

The Union had a large lounging area, with clusters of sofas and chairs for students to congregate, and here Crissy, Anh, and I waited. We pulled out our paper-bag lunches and nibbled away at our olive loaf sandwiches and almost-Oreo cookies. We played hangman and tic-tac-toe with my new pen and pad of paper. Anh broke into the Handi-Snacks Cheez 'N Crackers she had bought, which came with a flat red stick to spread the orange gooey cheese. She gave me half a cracker in exchange for a small palmful of M&M's.

Soon Crissy grew bored and wandered back to the bookstore. We followed her, of course, and there she made the discovery: *Playboy* magazine. The three of us huddled together to see gigantic breasts lunging toward us. Then Crissy picked up a copy of *Playgirl,* and gave me my first glimpse of a naked man. I remember the men in the photos as deeply unattractive. Some had grizzly beards, others looked slouched and round, with altogether too much body hair. One man sat with his legs splayed out, pulling on his penis, which he had somehow knotted into itself. Another wore a green football jersey and white athletic socks and nothing else. I remember thinking the whole arrangement looked uncomfortable. Feet covered, crotch laid bare. Then Crissy slid the magazine under her shirt. "You there," a voice called—the store clerk. Crissy dropped the *Playgirl* back into her hands, casually, without fear.

At home, we would have gotten in trouble just for saying the words "naked man." The images (naughty, we knew; bad, we knew) became a shared secret, a ripple of conspired rebellion, and I only wished that Crissy had been able to steal the magazine so the three of us could giggle together all over again. But when I mentioned this to her she just snorted at me. Whatever moment I had shared with my sisters in that bookstore had vanished.

I think it was that fall when Crissy's father reappeared. He had been a mystery, a white man whom Rosa had dated just long enough to get pregnant and earn the contempt of her family. This man's name, like my own mother's name, was never spoken. They were silent shames, aberrations that threatened to disrupt our household. Crissy hadn't seen him since she was almost too young to remember, and now he was going to take her to meet his parents in Mount Pleasant. She had never met them, or her half-sister. She had, it seemed, a whole other family out there. I wondered how the visit had been arranged: a hushed-up phone call; Rosa and my father concluding that they could not, after all, keep Crissy from knowing her real father. But they said nothing about it. The knowledge of this white man coming to sweep Crissy away simply absorbed into our minds as if through telepathy. So we waited, and swept and vacuumed, polishing the glass-topped table in the living room. We put on our favorite dresses and jumpers and patted down Vinh's little-boy hair with water. As we prepared, I pretended it was my and Anh's mother who was coming for a visit. It was she who was sending our household into a flurry of dusting and tidying. It was for her that I would choose my purple-striped dress and wait primly in the living room.

I imagined a huge, glamorous life for Crissy's father based on the facts of his whiteness and that he lived near the big city of Detroit. I imagined him dancing her away like Daddy Warbucks with Little Orphan Annie. Waiting for his arrival, I watched Crissy brush her hair extra hard. She parted it in the middle and clipped back both sides with matching barrettes. I was conscious of wanting to make a good impression, too, for Crissy's sake and for our own. I wanted to show her father that we were a good family.

When he arrived he made the living room small with his tall-ness, with his brown suit and striped tie. He was balding, and his ashen face had an expression I knew from my books to be a gri-mace. He stood near the entryway, clearly anxious not to linger. He had no interest in paying attention to Anh or me or anyone in our house. Our fresh dresses were an embarrassment of effort. Too soon, he and Crissy were gliding away in a dark sedan I couldn't identify from the living room window. All that weekend I summoned up images from the *Annie* movie. I thought of pil-lars, marble floors, glossy tap-dancing shoes. I had never been to Mount Pleasant, Michigan, but who wouldn't want to live there, on a mountain of pleasantness?

It was only an overnight visit, but a part of me felt afraid that we would not see Crissy again. Wouldn't I, if presented with the option, choose Daddy Warbucks's mansion over Florence Street? But Crissy returned as scheduled on Sunday afternoon, dropped off by her father in front of our house. She looked tired and list-less and she volunteered little information. Anh and I pestered her with questions. What were her grandparents like? Old. What was their house like? Nice. What was her half-sister's name? Danielle. What was she like? Nice but kinda hyper. What did they have for dinner? Here Crissy perked up a little as she de-scribed green peppers stuffed with ground beef and tomatoes. Was it delicious? I asked. She said it was. It certainly sounded fancy to me—maybe one of the fanciest dishes I had ever heard of. A vegetable doubling as a receptacle, a shell—food within food. I pictured a green pepper arranged in the middle of a floral-edged plate, the ball of ground beef tucked inside and drizzled with tomato sauce. I pictured an old white woman in a flowered housedress, mounding the raw meat with her pink, wrinkled hands. Crissy explained how her grandmother placed the peppers in a large, shallow baking pan; while they baked she set the table with a tablecloth, and place mats, and a full set of utensils at every place. I felt I knew exactly what those stuffed peppers tasted like, though I had never heard of such a thing until that moment. They were access to a new concept of how real people lived.

While I was dreaming of stuffed peppers, Anh wanted to know what Crissy's father thought of us. Crissy shrugged, indicating, *Nothing*. But then she laughed to herself. "Oh," she said, pointing at me. "He said you were homely."

I didn't know what the word meant, exactly, but I felt it lodging into the center of my chest. Crissy's laugh, the derision in her voice, made plain the meaning. When I looked it up later in the dictionary at the school library, angry tears sprang to my eyes. Why did I care what this white man thought of me? And more importantly, why did I have to be homely? I had failed to present a pretty household, and that failure was my own face. Innate, unchangeable. I *was* homely. A sad, spectacled spectacle, a sorry excuse for a stepsister. For years that word stayed with me, keeping me in my place when I ached to join the club of girlhood. I struggled to accept it. I had not, after all, typical princess goals of being the fairest of them all. I had never been good with putting makeup on dolls. I had never thought of myself as even passably good-looking. I was not in denial about my ugly, thick glasses and helmeted hair. My goal had always been to be the smartest, and I knew that smart and pretty didn't go together. Anh and Crissy, on the other hand, *were* pretty, and in that common bond grew an entire adolescence. They weren't just in the club; they were the club. They could do each other's hair for hours on end. They both seemed to know exactly which top matched with which skirt, how to apply eyeliner, how to paint nails, and, as they grew older, how to dress as near to Madonna's style as possible. If I attempted to braid my hair like theirs or tried a new combination of T-shirt and pants they would laugh in my face and literally shut me out, closing the bathroom door with a bang.

Fast-forward two years to 1984 and Crissy's fourteenth summer. She had a crush on Jeff Timmer, who lived just up Sycamore Street and was a junior in high school. She and Lisa (Keri and her family had moved out of state) spent all day walking past his house, hoping he would emerge so they could watch him mow the lawn.

Back at home, two boys started hanging out in our front yard, waiting for Crissy. Bobby, a comedian, was chubby and wore glasses, while Kenny looked and carried himself like Matt Dillon in *The Outsiders*. They both adored Crissy and she got a kick out of making fun of them. One time she accidentally ran over Bobby's glasses with his own bicycle. He didn't seem to mind. He cradled the broken frame in his hands, squinting his way back home. I liked Bobby and Kenny because they were nice to Anh and Vinh and me. They often accompanied us the mile and a half to Gas City to buy candy. Once in a great while, if I had enough funds, I would splurge on an ice cream sandwich pulled from the frosty freezer case. Crissy would nudge Bobby and Kenny to buy her Gobstoppers and Skittles. She had a ruthless attitude toward money and had no compunction about taking any that she found. By found I mean stole. She regularly sneaked money from Rosa's purse. And she knew all of my hiding spots: my coat pockets; an envelope shoved between my sheet and mattress; the hollowed-out space on the underside of the white unicorn statuette I kept on the dresser. I sometimes threw a fit when I discovered a stash of money missing, but mostly I just accepted my fate: powerless. Even my parents didn't seem too concerned whenever I tattled. "Stop doing that," was all they said to her.

I knew that the four years that separated me and Crissy were the difference between being a child and being a girl. A real girl, like Crissy, was what I could only hope to become one day. Upon getting initiated into the club—not like the stupid clubs I made up with Jennifer—I would learn the sacred truths about Boys and Hair and Makeup and Clothes.

Yet the rules seemed to be different for Anh. On the summer day she blocked me from the bathroom, then and there ending the baths we had always taken together, I knew she had gotten a pass to move forward. I was almost seven years old then, and Anh only eight, but it was clear that she'd made her choice to ally with our stepsister, to share a mirror and the perennial question: "How do I look?"

I realized that Crissy and Kenny were girlfriend and boyfriend when Bobby stopped showing up. I'd see Kenny lounging in the basement, his hair all feathered and mulleted, listening to Duran Duran. When Rosa caught wind of this she forbade him from stepping foot in the house again. She told my father and he yelled at Crissy, "No boys!" *Trouble* was the word they used. Meaning ruin and humiliation. Peril, a cyclone of doom. But in cautioning against trouble they invited it. Crissy drew herself up, undeterred. She would not be locked down in the house with a bunch of little kids. She disappeared for long afternoons, though I might see evidence of her in an empty plate streaked with honey, sitting in the kitchen sink. Her friend Keri wrote her letters from

Ohio and I peeked at one. *Have you ever been fingered?* she asked.

Crissy's hair was getting bigger, curlier, bangs poufier. She fought with our parents, defiantly raising the boom box volume to Def Leppard singing, *F-f-f-foolin'*. To Anh and me she'd drop blithe references to "the mall" and produce an astonishing array of bold new earrings, clothes, and makeup in hues of fuchsia and peacock blue. When I asked her how much it all cost she smiled without answering.

That summer I joined a Brownie troop with my friends from Ken-O-Sha. Even though the other girls were straight-up Grand Rapidian—proper and Dutch, from good clean homes—I knew at least this was an easier club to get into. So I looked forward to the meetings with Debora, the pretty blond troop leader who had a little boy named Cameron. I thought his name grand, high-class sounding, and was impressed by Debora's two-bedroom apartment with its white carpet and queenlike wicker chair in the living room. That's where Debora sat during the meetings, which I recall nothing about except the Grasshopper cookies and punch that we took turns bringing. Cameron's father wasn't around, and the circumstances of his absence were as murky to me as that of Crissy's father.

We met once a month to cross-stitch, or go on walks, and once we took a tour of Debora's workplace. She prepped frozen meals for Gordon Food Services, and had a stash of paper toques to wear. Her work uniform was all white. She explained how the meals she made would end up in hotels and restaurants all over the state. On our brief visit to the Gordon Foods kitchen I marveled at the stainless steel shelves stacked with cans and boxes. The environment was both sterile and chaotic—part hospital, part factory, part grocery store. I wondered how it was possible to make everything exactly the same for every tray of lasagna or turkey tetrazzini.

On one of our meetings we went to Ken-O-Sha to explore the nature trails that wound around Plaster Creek behind the school. Later, in sixth grade, we would learn how to identify trees, and what the different layers of soil were called, and take the lower grades on guided tours. It was late summer, and the air was just starting to carry a note of autumn's approach as Debora led us toward the entrance of the trail. In the near distance we saw a group of kids—older kids, junior high or maybe even high school—sitting on hoods of cars in the parking lot. Everyone knew that kids who hung out in the parking lot on weekends and after school were bad. They probably smoked and did drugs out there, and they would beat you up, or worse, if you got in their way. A nervous pall fell over the group as we walked beyond the kids' line of vision. "Don't worry, girls," Debora said. "God will protect us. That is," she added, "if you believe. If you don't believe, well . . ." Her voice faded meaningfully. I knew—everyone must have known—that the words were meant for me. Brownie troop had its prayers every meeting, and I never participated. I didn't refuse or say a word against them—I simply abstained. As much as I longed to fit in, I just couldn't bring myself to fake prayer.

I said nothing, though my heart beat a little faster—with anger, but also fear at being isolated. Then I saw a familiar face in that group of kids in the parking lot. Crissy. We were far away from the group now, but I knew her hair, her stance, her smile.

She was laughing at something, lifting a cigarette to her lips. A jolt of humiliation rushed through me and I wondered if the other girls had recognized her. Would they kick me out of the troop? Who would want to be friends with a heathen girl whose sister smoked and did drugs with bad boys in the parking lot?

It was Anh who finally let me know how Crissy got such stylish clothes and jewelry. "Duh," she said. "She steals them." She would bring a whole bunch of outfits into a dressing room to try on, Anh explained, and leave wearing as much as she could fit under her regular clothes. Earrings and makeup she slipped into her pockets. She did this all over Woodland and Eastbrook malls. "She showed me how," Anh boasted, admiring Crissy's ingenuity.

Part of me admired it, too—the illicit spoils, the brazenness, the fact that Crissy always got what she wanted. But my overriding thought was *trouble*. Police, getting arrested, going to jail, her permanent record. I blamed my parents. Why couldn't they lay off her case? She wouldn't have to steal if they gave her more money, I reasoned. I would have given her my own money gladly, forgetting any past thievery, if it would mean keeping her safe. Anh was confident in Crissy's shoplifting skills, but I couldn't shake the uneasy feeling I had. It was new, this worrying about her, since all my life I had feared Crissy's judgment and ridicule. I didn't know what to do but try to stay close to her, lingering when she sang along to "Sister Christian" and "Borderline" and sitting so near when we watched *Fame* on TV that she'd shove me away. "Quit it," she'd say.

❧

Just after the school year started, Debora presented Brownie badges at a mother-daughter lunch in a courtyard at Ken-O-Sha school. I didn't know what we had earned or learned, and half of us didn't even have Brownie uniforms to pin any badges on. I was bored with the whole idea of the troop by then, and dreaded the lunch as much as Rosa probably did. Debora had asked us each to bring a dish to share and our own plates, utensils, and drinks. Rosa and I brought corned beef and Colby cheese sandwiches and cans of Squirt. Others brought macaroni salad, Jell-O squares, bologna sandwiches, and juice boxes. As we sat on stone benches, Debora led the group in a prayer. I glanced at my stepmother, who bowed her head just slightly and said nothing when the others said, "Amen." I knew she thought of Brownie troop as an indulgence, a peer pressure thing. She must have been worried that I would immerse myself in such a group, perhaps become religious, too.

I noticed that Emily Voss had brought something in a round deep-dish pie pan. Her mother pulled back the tinfoil to reveal a blanket of mashed potatoes. "Shepherd's pie," Rosa exclaimed. I looked at her in surprise and she said, "Crissy loves shepherd's pie." This was news to me and I almost said, *Are you sure?* There was so much, it seemed, I didn't know about her. I had forgotten to bring forks, so I could only watch the others dig into the mashed potatoes. Underneath, like cake beneath frosting, a layer of ground beef revealed itself, and drops of gravy spotted Emily's plate. I watched the fork travel from her plate to her mouth, thinking that my corned beef sandwich tasted like construction paper.

All at once I felt exhausted with Brownie troop and the useless badges—something about being tidy and polite, and knowing how to use a compass—and the day seemed late in the sky, nearly over. It was weird to sit in this school courtyard on a Saturday, with the empty halls behind us. It was weird to be sitting here playing mother and daughter. Somewhere out in the teachers' parking lot, I imagined, Crissy was leaning against someone's car. She was smoking a cigarette, her stolen bracelets flashing on her arms. Debora had wanted me to be afraid, I realized, just as she had wanted me to believe what I could not believe. I was supposed to fear teenagers, boys, the wreck of adolescence. The thought of Crissy out there struck me as terribly lonesome. Oh, she had no shortage of friends, but she would always be the oldest sister, the one in charge. She would have to lead the way through growing up. She would always have to go first.

In my hand I balled up half a sandwich. The bread gave way easily, as it had in Crissy's hands when she had shown me how to eat rhubarb, bread, and honey. It melted into itself, returning to its pasty origins, the meat and cheese folding inside as easily as a tongue. In my mind I saw Crissy pushing off on her bicycle, riding fast around the corner.

I hated to acknowledge the end of summer, those suspended hours of drawing pictures with Jennifer while Anh hung out with a new girl down the street. Crissy talked on the phone, broke up with Kenny, brought home more clothes, more makeup. She stared in the mirror for hours. Vinh built Lincoln Log cabins with Jennifer's brother, the two of them blissfully exempt from the rules and travails of girlhood in Grand Rapids. Noi worked in the garden, shifting around her sprinklers that fanned to and fro in slow arcs. Our uncles came home from work and cranked up old Santana or the Guess Who. A golden haze settled over the neighborhood and I longed to keep it, to prevent the night from falling. Then our parents came home. They shut down the day, their very appearance signaling tension. A fight could erupt any second, aimed at any one of us. A sulk, a smart remark. *Wipe off that eye shadow. Be quiet. Don't talk back to me.*

Gone were the days of bread and honey, of following Crissy down the backyard hill to see where she would lead us. I was old enough to disobey her orders, and look at her with disquiet, and consider what kind of girls Anh, Crissy, and I might turn out to be. I was old enough to refuse without fear a stick of rhubarb, sanded with sugar and still warm from someone else's garden. But I was never offered it again.

Salt Pork

LIVING WITH THREE SIBLINGS, TWO UNCLES, A GRAND-
mother, and nosy parents meant that privacy was as impossible as
having my own refrigerator stocked with cheesecake, Otter Pops,
and pudding snacks. Even the bathroom, the only room with a
lock, provided little solace, since someone was always knocking
on the door and shouting, "Hurry up!" As the youngest ones, my
brother Vinh and I were entitled to the least amount of space.
We roamed the house looking for hideouts, building forts out
of cardboard and towels. We were powerless against Anh and
Crissy, who had control over dresser drawers, radio stations, and
which games we might play.

Deep in the heart of the 1980s, my sisters spent hours cho-
reographing dance moves to Pat Benatar and Scandal. *Shootin' at
the walls of heartache, bang bang! I am the warrior.* I tried to copy
them, afraid of missing out on the knowledge they held, but they
usually jeered me out of the room. I was left to admire from a
distance their moussed hair, their pouty, bored expressions, the
way they let their shirts dangle off one shoulder. They both had
the natural athletic grace I lacked, and earned first-place blue

ribbons on Field Day while I took home white ribbons marked "Participant." They could mimic Madonna's "Lucky Star" video right down to her deliberate blinks and serious, sexy frowns. They were experts at recording songs off the radio and every Sunday listened to Casey Kasem's weekly Top 40 countdown and long-distance dedications. In the mornings they daubed their eyelids with stripes of color and produced a magical supply of cool earrings—lightning bolts, gigantic plastic hoops. My ears refused to stay pierced, though I had gone twice to the gum-chewing girl with the piercing gun at Claire's in the mall. I shuddered at the crusty aftermath and the chore of rotating the studs each day. My earlobes rebelled, and both times I let the holes close up.

I had only one thing to call my own: I read. Reading was my privacy. I would beg Rosa to take me to the nearby public library branch, where the one coveted copy of *Are You There God? It's Me, Margaret* always had a long wait list. After snapping up whatever Judy Blume books I could find—*Deenie, Tales of a Fourth Grade Nothing*—I'd collect an armful of titles from the rest of the kids' section, sometimes so many that I couldn't carry them all. Rosa clicked her tongue at my greed and said that I'd better get through every last one before they were due. At least the books were free, I pointed out. I could spend whole weekends reading on my top bunk bed, with Jell-O Pops, Nutter Butters, and Chicken in a Biskit crackers swiped from the kitchen. I carried books with me everywhere, even to the Dairy Cone. They were a safety, a just-in-case. Some people have imaginary friends; I had characters in books.

Twice a year at Ken-O-Sha Elementary, each student got to pick out two free books from RIF, Reading Is Fundamental.

Outside the principal's office, the row of white-clothed tables laden with paperbacks would make my heart jump. Running my hands over the shiny covers, I would take too long to make up my mind. I had nightmares about being sick at home and missing the RIF days. A few times a year we could also order books and magazines through *Scholastic* catalogs that the teachers handed out. Rarely did Rosa let me order a book, or allow me to use some of my Christmas and Tet money to buy them. She said that libraries existed for a reason and that buying books, things that were only to be read once, was a waste even though I had a habit of rereading them. Rosa also had a thing about books lying around—she thought it was tacky, that books should be kept out of sight, especially if company was coming over. Unable to stay organized, I ended up losing books under the bed and behind dressers, racking up late fees at the library, until my father built a small white bookshelf for the hallway.

I liked to pile my books around me in bed, moatlike, and sleep among the narratives. *Ramona Quimby, Encyclopedia Brown, The Great Brain, Mrs. Piggle-Wiggle. Choose Your Own Adventure, Charlie and the Chocolate Factory, Charlotte's Web, The Cay, The Secret Garden, The Chronicles of Narnia.* Then writers like Cynthia Voigt, Richard Peck, Norma Fox Mazer. I lingered over my favorite food parts—descriptions of Turkish Delight, fried chicken, hamburgers with onions, thick hot chocolate, even the beef tongue the Quimby family once had for dinner. I liked stories of kids on the outside, on the margins, overlooked. *The Pinballs. The Homecoming. Jacob Have I Loved. A Girl Called Al.* And then on to the shelf called Literature. *Jane Eyre, Wuthering Heights, Little Women, A Tale of Two Cities.* Old-fashioned language, and reading it felt like a wriggling down into some tunnel of words. I was determined to fit in, to learn how to see in that dark.

I read to be alone. I read so as not to be alone.

When I stepped into the brown-tiled entryway of the Kentwood Public Library, the sunlight flowing down on me from the high windows, I felt a sense of importance. It gratified me to be in a place devoted to books and quiet; I was filled with a sense of hope. Reading to me *was* fundamental, as fundamental as food. And nothing could be more satisfying than reading a good book while eating a good meal of *mi* soup, french fries, and a thin cut of steak. I plowed through books as fast as possible in order to read them again.

I loved the opening of Louisa May Alcott's *Little Women*, when the March girls give away their Christmas breakfast to a poor German family and Mr. Laurence sends over a surprise bounty of bon bons, ice cream, cake, and hothouse flowers. Then Jo makes friends with Laurie, bringing him a bowl of beautiful blancmange. A few chapters later, she struggles over wilted lobster salad and accidentally salts rather than sugars a dish of plump strawberries drowning in cream. The Marches were a romantic ideal with their white gloves and snug evenings, their plays and art and moral lessons from Marmee. I felt inspired to be like Jo, with her pluck and ingenuity; whether up in the garret or among the family circle, she was like a mythical heroine to me.

More down to earth was Beverly Cleary's heroine Ramona Quimby, one of my closest fictional friends. I understood her dread of having the same dull after-school snack of juice and rye crisp the same way I understood her resentment toward pretty, blond-curled Willa Jean next door. My favorite Quimby meal takes place at the Whopperburger, when a nice old gentleman secretly pays for their dinner. I appreciated the realism of how the Quimbys worried about money. Mr. Quimby loses his job, takes up smoking, goes back to school, then works as a grocery store cashier. When the cat eats half of their family jack-o'-lantern, Mrs. Quimby converts the leftover pumpkin into soups and breads. The family makes ends meet. In spite of such tensions I never doubted the Quimbys' love for one another. I would gladly have traded my life with Ramona's, to live on Klickitat Street in Oregon, with the hump of Mount Hood just visible in the distance on a clear day. I would have liked a mother like Mrs. Quimby, who could be stern but never mean, and who always seemed to understand the small and big anxieties that make up the life of a girl.

All of my fictional friends liked to eat, but perhaps no one did more than Laura Ingalls Wilder. For the Ingalls family out on the plains and prairies, every harvest means a year of leanness or a year of fullness. The long days of sowing and haying and threshing could be distilled into a single sourdough biscuit fresh from Ma's oven. The days provide slices of salt pork, purchased in town then parboiled, dipped in flour, and fried in their own fat. The days mean fighting against blackbirds that ravaged the corn and oats. Once, Ma gathers the blackbirds to make a pie. "The meat was so tender that it slipped from the bones," writes Wilder. "There's no great loss without some small gain," says Ma.

The first book in the series, *Little House in the Big Woods*, was given to me by Jennifer Vander Wal on my ninth birthday. My first reaction to it was disdain; I was beyond illustrations and stories that began with the words "Once upon a time." I had, too, an automatic suspicion of any book endorsed by the Vander Wals. So I set it aside, unread, for months. But then the boredom of winter got to me, and one Saturday afternoon I read the book from beginning to end, caught up in the butter and bacon, and how every mealtime depended on the success of Pa's hunting or Ma's gardening. I felt a stab of regret at having gone so long without knowing about hog-butchering, maple-sugar-making, cheese-making, and sausage-making; I had lost years of pork cracklings, hulled corn, and hot johnnycakes. When Pa butchers his hog, he blows up its bladder into a ball so Mary and Laura can play with it. Then Ma lets them roast the pig's tail. They hold it before a blazing fire, watching the curlicue get crackly and greasy, then nibble at the bits of meat that Ma sprinkles with salt. In the winter Pa shoots a bear in the woods and keeps the meat frozen in the attic. Then there's the sugaring-off dance at Grandma and Grandpa's, to celebrate making the year's supply of maple sugar. Laura and Mary pour hot syrup onto plates of fresh snow, making squiggle shapes that "hardened at once and were candy. . . . They could eat all they wanted, for maple candy never hurt anybody."

I was thrilled when Laura slapped her sister Mary. She had a good reason. Mary was showing off her blond hair, letting Laura know that it was the prettiest of all and that no one cared for brown hair like Laura's. It was a dull, dirt brown, Laura admitted, and knowing it "swelled her throat tight." So she slapped Mary, and that's when I thought, I could like this girl. The older Laura grew, the smarter, sassier, and more likable she became. She, too, has a blond-haired nemesis, Nellie Oleson, who sniffs at her and calls her "country folk." And Laura never stints on food. The scraping of butter on a dry slice of toast merits her attention as much as a holiday feast of roasted jackrabbit, bread-and-onion stuffing, rich brown gravy, and dried-apple pie. She loves lettuce leaves sprinkled with sugar, cold cottage cheese balls, and the first spring chicken, fried and served with creamed potatoes and new peas. She glories in a birthday party where the hostess served oyster soup, fried mashed potato cakes, hot creamy codfish balls, and white cake with a whole orange for each guest. When she describes a barrel of lemonade, the "lemon slices floating thick" in cold, sweetened well water, I longed to try out the communal dipper, all the better to wash down Ma's bread-and-butter sandwiches and Pa's "boughten" treat of smoked herring.

Farmer Boy, which follows Almanzo Wilder's boyhood in New York State, goes even crazier with food. Where the Ingallses count pennies and ration potatoes, the prosperous Wilders eat hearty piles of meat and beans every night. The breadth of their everyday breakfasts astound: thick oatmeal covered with cream, sausage cakes, pancakes and syrup, fried potatoes, jellies, preserves, and bread, and slices of apple pie with melted cheese. The lunch pail the Wilder children bring to school holds delectable bread and butter and sausages, fresh apples, doughnuts, and spiced apple turnovers. At dinner, Almanzo can count on ham or roast beef or chicken pie, mashed potatoes with gravy, baked beans with a bit of "quivering" salt pork, mashed turnips and stewed pumpkin, watermelon pickles and jelly and bread and butter, and bird's nest pudding with spiced cream poured right over it. Then, after evening chores are done, the family sits cozily together munching apples, cider, doughnuts, and freshly popped popcorn. The girls do embroidery work or read from the newspaper; the boys grease their shoes and whittle. Mother Wilder knits jackets and caps. Her hands—like all good mothers' hands—never cease moving. On Sundays everyone eats stacks of her pancakes, richly layered with butter and maple sugar, and looks forward to chicken pie after church. At Christmas, the family table includes roasted goose with "edges of dressing curling out," a suckling pig with an apple stuck in its mouth, candied carrots, fried apples and onions, all manner of mashed parsnips, squash, and potatoes, and an assortment of fruit preserves and pickles and jelly to go with cornbread and wheat bread and light white bread. Waiting for his serving, Almanzo laments: "Spoons ate up the clear cranberry jelly, and gouged deep into the mashed potatoes, and ladled away the brown gravies." Then, of course, there are fruitcakes and pies—apple, mincemeat, custard, pumpkin, and vinegar. In my favorite Garth Williams illustration in *Farmer Boy*, Almanzo is cramming his mouth with a giant forkful of food while half a ham and a pie sit nearby, ready to be devoured. Almanzo is hungry on nearly every page of the book, and his hunger matches his ambition to be a better farmer, and thus breadwinner, than anyone else. And so he is depicted as the right companion for Laura. He knows how to raise the finest horses and grow the fattest pumpkins; he knows how to make buckwheat pancakes soaked in molasses and butter. He knows the value of food, and risks his life to go after a crop of wheat in the middle of the Hard Winter, to keep the town of De Smet from starving.

Laura was born in the Big Woods of Wisconsin in 1867, a few years before the Ingalls family began their migration westward. They lived in parts of Missouri, Kansas (Indian Territory), Minnesota, and Iowa before settling in Dakota Territory (De Smet, South Dakota) in 1879. Like her father, Laura has an itchy wandering foot, a desire to keep pushing on to see what lands lie beyond the horizon. But sensible, strict Ma, a former school-teacher, had long ago made her husband promise to settle down so her girls could get an education and become teachers, too. Ma and Mary frequently got on my nerves. They were so ladylike all the time, so disciplined about chore time. My dislike for Ma was cemented in her dislike of Indians, whom she called "howling savages." I knew that if I had lived in De Smet she would never have let Laura consort with me. Still, I tried to keep in mind Ma's good points. She was, for instance, a domestic goddess. She could stew rabbit and dumplings over an open fire in the middle of a prairie, braid straw hats, and sew complicated dresses and dolls with ease and expertise. During the Hard Winter of 1880 she contrives sustenance from their dwindling supply of flour, beans, and potatoes, saving a morsel of salted cod to break the monotony of plain brown bread. For dinner, which meant lunch, Ma might cook up a hot bean soup, flavored with a bit of salt pork. Then she'd drain the beans, lace them with molasses, and set them in the oven with the same salt pork to make baked beans for supper.

Ma had the cooking skills, but I preferred Pa Ingalls's company. He could hunt birds, rabbits, and deer; he could make fish traps; he knew just what it meant to see that muskrats had built themselves an extra-thick home for winter. Pa has an intuitive understanding of geography, climate, and behavior. He gets along with Indians, too, and *Little House on the Prairie* makes clear that his friendship with the Osage chief Soldat du Chene is the only thing that saves the family and the other settlers in the area from being killed. While Mary is Ma's daughter, Laura is Pa's. Together they find fright and fascination in wolves and wild animals. They ponder buffalo wallows, watch the laying of west-ward train rails, and make fast friends with the tobacco-spitting "Tennessee wildcat" Mr. Edwards.

Every time the Ingallses move they have to break new sod and start a new farm from scratch. So the family has to rely, increas-ingly, on salt pork bought from a store in town. Salt pork is always described as fatty and white, "held down in brine." It represents both failure and prosperity: a failure to produce a hardy, self-sustaining farm that included fresh pork; a prosperity that allowed the purchase of meat from the store. Bacon was one of my favor-ite foods; I liked it super crisp, the grease perfuming my hands. After I read the *Little House* books I began to pretend that bacon was salt pork and that I was Laura herself. She was short and small like me, and she savored every last touch of the salt on her tongue. Such a moment might be her only pleasure of the day. I imagined she secretly longed for meals to last and for the salt pork slices never to end, that she fantasized about frying a few slices just for herself in the middle of the day, watching the white fat darken.

But gluttony was a sin, and nothing was worse than wasted food, which was wasted work. A pioneer in a covered wagon had to keep a careful eye on the provisions, gauge how much to eat and how much to save for the rutted path ahead. The goal of settling was farming, creating an independent cycle of crops, livestock, and vegetable gardens. The Ingallses struggle against storms, bad weather, stubborn soil, even plagues of grasshoppers, always trying to pull ahead and usually getting pushed back. Which is why a long day of plowing the fields could be bright-ened by a spoonful of ginger flavoring the water jug. The troubles garnered by a too-small crop could be forgotten for an evening with a surprise pie made from green pumpkin.

In many ways, their pioneer life reminded me of immigrant life. As they search for new homesteads, they, too, experience isolation and the scramble for shelter, food, work, and a place to call home. In the opening scene of *Little House on the Prairie* the Ingallses say good-bye to their family in Wisconsin, and the finality is chilling. They don't know if they will ever see each other again. Without mail or telephones, the rest of the family is left wondering for months what happened—if they survived, if they were okay, where they had ended up. The book's quiet description of good-byes belies the great anxiety of westward migration. As the Ingallses travel in their wagon, looking for their last stop, they meet settlers from Norway, Sweden, Germany. "They're good neighbours," Pa says. "But I guess our kind of folks is pretty scarce." Yet these European immigrant families would one day cease to be foreign and become "our kind of folks." Like the Ingallses, they would blend in, become American, eventually refer to their ancestry as something fond and distant. "Trust a Scotchwoman to manage," Pa says admiringly of Ma. The children of European immigrants would be able to answer the question "Where are you from?" with "Out East," or "Wisconsin," or "Minnesota," and no one would say, "No, I mean where are you *really* from?"

The Ingallses were the epitome of American. They memorized the Declaration of Independence, knew an inexhaustible number of hymns and American folk songs, and took pride in being "free and independent." They had big, "Westward Ho!" ideas about migration, property, and ownership. They built homes everywhere they landed, frying up salt pork in their iron skillet in hand-built hearths across the plains. They had such confidence in the building, such righteous belief in the idea of home, in the right to land, in the life of farming.

As I grew older, I had an increasingly uneasy time reading the books. The Ingallses were a pious group; they loved church, knew the Bible inside and out, and sometimes reminded me uncomfortably of the Vander Wals and all the other hard-core Christians I had encountered in Grand Rapids. Then there was the issue of racism. Not just Ma Ingalls's hatred of Indians, which persisted no matter what Pa said. In *Little House in the Big Woods* the family sings a song about "a little darky." In *Little Town on the Prairie* Pa and a group of men folk put on blackface and perform a vaudeville show for the town. "Look at those darkies' feet," they sing, prancing around stage. "Those darkies can't be beat!" I knew that people like me would also have been considered outcasts, heathens, and strangers; we didn't even count.

In a way, it makes sense that I would become enamored with a literature so symbolic of manifest destiny and white entitlement. I didn't have any nonwhite literature, anyway, to know what else I could become. My favorite books, the ones I gravitated to, were as white or as Anglo as a person could get. Though my relationship with the Ingalls family and other white characters grew complicated, I had a strong reserve of denial, an ability to push away the unpleasant parts. For I had created, if somewhat unknowingly, a group portrait of protagonists—girls I wished I could be. Girls as capable as Laura Ingalls, as talented as Jo March, as smart and privileged as Louise Fitzhugh's Harriet the Spy.

Harriet Welsch spent all of her time taking notes on people. She listened at windows and doors and hid in dumbwaiters, putting together profiles of people in her neighborhood—the rich and ridiculous Agatha K. Plumber, the cat-loving Harrison Withers, the always-hungry delivery boy at the Dei Santi grocery who could eat pounds of cheese, bread, and tomatoes in one sitting. Harriet wanted to be a writer, and had stacks of notebooks filled with her uncensored, critical thoughts about everyone she met or saw. As the only child to rich parents, Harriet had her own room and bathroom. She had a governess, Ole Golly, to look after her, and a cook to feed her cake and milk every day after school. In short, Harriet had an envied life, and part of that came from her freedom to write. I tried to capture that same independence. Because Harriet loved tomato sandwiches, describing how her mouth watered at the thought of the creamy mayonnaise and ripe red tomatoes, I tried to like them, too. When I wrote like Harriet, I took pleasure in the release of opinions and the scrawling of thoughts that could not be said out loud for fear of getting laughed at, teased, or in trouble. These entries ranged from hating my sister for taking the last Chicken Coop drumstick to wondering if unicorns existed somewhere, and if they did, what it would be like to have one.

I kept a pure diary of unfettered thoughts—in which the risk of another reader isn't present—for about a week, which was about the time it took my sisters and stepmother to locate and read what I had written. Rosa frequently searched our bedroom dressers to read our diaries, which she herself had given us for Christmas, not even pretending to conceal her intentions. She believed that everything we did and wrote was hers, since we lived under her roof; she was worried that if she didn't monitor us we would become wayward and bad. She often spoke vaguely of "bad girls" and how important it was not to become one of them.

Anh and Crissy were often bored enough to dip into my diary, too, and enjoyed laughing at my fanciful unicorn dreams and bitter thoughts about clothes and dinners I couldn't have. I knew I had to either stop keeping a diary altogether or find a way to keep a truly private one. The former wouldn't hold—I was too restless and introverted—and the latter proved impossible. In such a small house, no hiding place could go undiscovered. I slid the diary between shirts in my dresser, pushed it inside my pillowcase, tucked it under the fitted sheet that nestled against the wall. Inevitably Anh, Crissy, or Rosa would find the diary or catch me pulling it out. My next stop was to foil them. *Stop reading my diary and go away!* I wrote in block letters on the first full page. I filled the next several pages with fake entries—dull ramblings about sledding and snow, descriptions of what my dolls were doing with their afternoons. Then I turned the book upside down and flipped to the back to write my real entries. But my stepmother and sisters were as persistent as I was. Harriet, I knew, would have understood my pain; when her classmates discovered her notebooks they ostracized her.

But at least Harriet had a pretty bedroom all her own. Her house was big enough to have a library and a grand sweeping staircase. After her spy route Harriet would go to her favorite soda fountain and order a ten-cent egg cream. She had the kind of wealth and privilege I wished that I could take for granted. Her father worked in television and used the word *fink* a lot. Her mother was slender and attractive and left a romantic trail of perfume when she went off to a party, while Harriet stayed at home with the wise, intuitive Ole Golly, who quoted Whitman and Wordsworth and knew how to cook lobster thermidor.

It was a wonderful suspension of self to pretend to be Harriet and immerse myself in her New York life. But I knew she was as out of reach as Laura Ingalls. I could never have a socialite mother like Mrs. Welsch, or an expert in domesticity like Ma Ingalls, or even someone like Mrs. Quimby, who worked a part-time job and sympathized with her daughter's desires and frustrations. Certainly a mother as upstanding and goddesslike as Marmee March was out of the question. Reading these books was the same as reading fantasy. Girls like Jennifer Vander Wal and Holly Jansen could legitimately pretend to be Anne of Green Gables or Jo March, but a Vietnamese girl like me could never even have lived near them. Nonetheless, drawn to what I could not have, I kept seeking out landscapes in which I could not have existed. Deep down, I thought I could prove that I could be a more thorough and competent white girl than any of the white girls I knew. I gave my dolls and stuffed animals names like Polly, Vanessa, Elspeth, and Anastasia. I pursued all the British books on the library's Literature shelf, working to understand the language and cadence of *Great Expectations, The Return of the Native,* and *Pride and Prejudice,* though I often came away feeling moody and dissatisfied, a cloud coming over the landscape of my imagination. I spent several months trying to speak in a British accent—modeling it on Julie Andrews's in *Mary Poppins* and Hayley Mills's in *Pollyanna*—and used it at home whenever my sisters spoke to me. I made myself over into the whitest girl possible. No doubt this contributed to the quick erosion of my Vietnamese. I thought if I could know inside and out how my heroines lived and what they ate and what they loved—Harriet in New York, Laura in Dakota, Jo March in Massachusetts, Elizabeth Bennet in England—I could be them, too. I could read my way out of Grand Rapids.

12

Holiday Tamales

MY STEPMOTHER GOT HER HIGH SCHOOL GRADUATION photo taken a year after she started college. In the picture, her face is framed by a coiffed 'do that curves in big commas at her jawline. Her lips and cheeks have been shaded pink in the style of the time and you can tell she's the kind of girl who wears cat-eye glasses strung on a chain around her neck. *What was it like?* I used to ask Rosa about growing up in Fruitport, going to high school in the sixties and having nine brothers and sisters. If she felt like answering, she'd describe a life that I had imagined only from books: feeding chickens, washing dirty clothes with a hand-held scrub board, having no electricity or running water for years. She'd had a formal picture taken in her senior year of high school but couldn't bear how she looked in her handmade, made-over outfit. So after she had attended a year at Grand Valley State she sat for the real portrait, the image of herself she wanted to capture.

The drive from Grand Rapids to Fruitport takes about forty-five minutes, but when I was a kid it seemed to last an entire day. Nothing in the landscape changed—just the same birch and pine trees planted in the median, the same green exit signs pointing the way to the towns like Nunica and Holland. I knew that Lake Michigan lay just beyond Fruitport, tantalizingly near yet nowhere in sight. My siblings and I clamored to go to the beach at P. J. Hoffmaster State Park and my father dreamed about speedboats, but we only visited the lake during summer trips to see Rosa's family. Vinh's birth had brought her back into the fold, and just like that our family grew. Crissy jumped in with open arms—they were her blood, after all—but Anh and I hesitated, overwhelmed by the great number of people we were suddenly supposed to claim as our aunts, uncles, and cousins. My father appeared to endure the visits with unusual quietude. Noi and my uncles almost always stayed home. We were, from the beginning, divided.

Rosa's parents, Juan and Maria, had both grown up in Texas—Juan in San Antonio, Maria in Brownsville. They met on the migrant trail, working their way up to Michigan for the cherry and sugarbeet seasons. Maria had entered a convent at thirteen, but left three years later, when her mother died in childbirth, to take care of her six younger siblings. As the oldest, her role as matriarch began early. After she and Juan married and began to have kids he took a job as a *toquero* in Saginaw. He drove truckloads of fruit and vegetables from the farms to the distributors, and his easy translations between English and Spanish, along with his affable manner, made him an ideal go-between to negotiate wages and terms. Rosa was still a little girl when the family settled in Fruitport, where her father started working at a foundry. Finally, the family began building their house. There were ten kids now and they spent that first year in the basement, the only part of the house that was done. They had no electricity yet, so the days stretched out dark and dank. They used hurricane lamps and propane heaters. Maria cooked over the portable gas stove she had used for years in the migrant camps. Slowly Juan finished the rest of the house, a long ranch style on a few acres of wooded land. It had electricity and a real bathroom—no more bathing on Saturdays in a tin tub with water pumped by hand and heated on the stove. But washing clothes was still a dreaded chore: scrub the dirtiest clothes on the tin scrub board; put the rest of the clothes through the washer-wringer, twice; clip everything to dry on the clotheslines outside; carefully iron and fold. Rosa's mother sewed almost all of her children's clothes, and what she couldn't make herself she bought at secondhand stores.

In the summers, Grandma and Grandpa, as Anh and I were instructed to call them, threw huge barbecues, cooking slabs of meat on giant grills fashioned out of oil drums. The men of the family would gather around the grill with cans of Budweiser. The smoke obscured their expressions but not their big laughs, the jokes they told in Spanish that I wished I could understand. Rosa kept trying to teach us the language through immersion techniques. *Buenas noches, Ándale,* and *Cállate la boca* had become part of our vocabulary. Though I generally considered myself pretty quiet, I heard that last one a lot. I tried to keep these phrases under wraps from my friends. They thought I was different enough with the whole Vietnamese thing; adding Mexican American to the mix just put me over the edge.

Rosa's family was enormous: I now had dozens of cousins, and all these *tías* and *tíos* to keep track of. As with the Vietnamese parties, the women, men, and kids generally split into their own groups, each having its own leader. The kids played tag and hide-and-seek in the summer and went sledding in the winter. The men drank beer and watched the Tigers or the Lions. Grandpa, a man of graceful movements and gentle laugh, played the guitar, and often sang lonesome Mexican songs he had learned growing up in San Antonio. It was said that all quartz watches stopped when he put them on his wrist. In the kitchen the women's voices rose and fell against each other, gossiping and quarreling like competing birds. Grandma was the terrifying matriarch, and her word was the word: if she declared that the arroz con pollo didn't need more salt, then it didn't.

I sussed out the nice aunts and uncles. The mean ones pinched our cheeks too hard and laughed, using Spanish phrases I didn't understand. The nice ones smiled at us and asked if we had gotten enough to eat; one aunt even made me a big floppy doll for Christmas. It took me a long time to realize that the doll was supposed to look like me, with black yarn hair and brown eyes. I named her Pollyanna.

I never embarked on a trip without a supply of books. They were my safety blanket, my stay against boredom, conversation, and interaction. Rosa's family, like my father's friends, had clear expectations about the role of children. Be seen but not heard, and do what you're told. Kids were servants and gofers, and if an adult told you to fetch a napkin or find his shoes, then you had better do it or suffer consequences: get yelled at in front of everybody, or worse, spanked with a belt. I saw kids get in trouble every time; they shouted too loudly when they won a game of checkers, they got in a fight with someone they accused of cheating, they rolled their eyes, showing "attitude," or they simply didn't eat everything on their plate.

I tried to keep a low profile. In school, I stayed safe by being good. At home, I stayed safe by being alone. The downside was a feeling of loneliness that I couldn't shake; I didn't, after all, want to be left out. I wanted to be a regular kid, too—jump rope (though I never could Double Dutch the way Anh could), play games, draw hopscotch lines in the dirt of the driveway. It just seemed that I could never do anything without getting in trouble or inviting ridicule. I began to realize that the problem was not my voice—I seldom spoke among Rosa's family—but my face. I wore a frown without meaning to. There was an impudence, a defiance in my expression. It drove Rosa and my father insane with anger sometimes. When I had no voice to explain why I didn't do my chores, my face, instead of showing submission, showed the opposite. *Don't you look at me like that,* my father often shouted. *You're cruisin' for a bruisin',* Rosa would add. Try as I might, I couldn't keep my rebellious feelings contained under a shell of trained impassivity. The thick, plastic-rimmed glasses Rosa had chosen for me didn't help my cause, either. I looked pathetic and trollish, and inspired irritation rather than pity. All the kids seemed too old or too young or too noisy for me; I wanted to be back at home with Noi, sharing a can of lychees and putting together a jigsaw puzzle. We could have the whole house to ourselves.

At Grandma and Grandpa's house I walked on tiptoe, feeling like a delinquent, waiting for a chance to relax. When everyone else was outside I studied the rosaries over the doorways, the giant reproduction of *The Last Supper* over the dining table, and the western scenes of Conestoga wagons printed on the living room upholstery. In the hallway leading to the bedroom, I memorized, out of pure boredom, the "footprints in the sand" story that had been framed on the wall. *And the Lord said, My son, dur-*

ing your times of suffering, when you could see only one set of foot-prints, it was then that I carried you.

I remember being caught in the hallway, looking at that footprints story, by Tía Ana, the youngest sister. It was her graduation party—this must have been the summer of 1984, when I was nine going on ten—and she was in such a good mood that she invited me into her room, where a bunch of cousins were helping her get ready. Ana wore a smocked, strapless white dress she kept adjusting. "How are my *chichones?*" she asked cousin Eva, who was a year older than Crissy and had a dimpled smile. Winking, Ana remarked that there would be a lot of boys at the party. Like her sisters, she had plump arms and lots of coarse, curly hair. I thought she was beautiful and happy, reaching out to claim the summer day as her own.

Rosa had been the first in the family to go to college. Most of the kids at Fruitport High didn't go, and Rosa herself never thought of it until a counselor approached her one day with the suggestion. Back then, Rosa later told me, no one thought about Mexicans going to college. The goal, after high school, was to get married. Men sought factory jobs. Women sought to be wives and mothers. A car, a house, and a family were the signs of success—a good, decent life. But the thought of college excited Rosa, who loved school and dreamed about traveling the world. She applied to a new college, Grand Valley State, located just twenty miles away in Allendale, Michigan, and the school offered her a scholarship. It was only then that Rosa told her parents about her plans.

Being the first to go, Rosa opened the way for her siblings to follow. Only one sister pursued it as far as Rosa did and even-tually moved to Colorado, the only one in the family to leave

Michigan. Others made it a semester or two before dropping out and returning home to marry and work. The fact was that a college education set Rosa apart. She was perceived as being "too big for her britches," a phrase she frequently applied to me, followed by, "Who do you think you are?" I wonder what the family thought when she arrived with her half-white daughter born out of wedlock, her new Vietnamese husband, two Vietnamese step-daughters, and her new half-Vietnamese son.

As much as I hadn't bargained for a whole new family, I did want to be accepted into the group. But as the visits to Rosa's family accumulated, so did my sense of self-consciousness. I was too ugly, my body too small, my face too stubborn. I was too aware of being Vietnamese. I was the quiet one in the corner with my books, the one who refused to be like the others. I couldn't conceal it, either. I didn't want to sit outside slapping mosquitoes and watching the men drink beer. I didn't want to fetch kitchen supplies for the women or listen to them laugh and comment, as I grew older, on my non-*chichona* status. My stepmother and her sisters had big curves and often talked about them, nudging and laughing, using a flurry of Spanish words that I supposed referred to various body parts, grown-up acts.

It didn't take long for my loneliness, though it was mostly self-imposed, to devolve into resentment. I resented the aunts and uncles who couldn't tell my sister and me apart. I resented long holidays in Fruitport, looking for a place to hide out with my books. I resented, then buried in guilt, being told to love people I did not know.

When my books had been read and reread, when all of the kids were as bored as can be—the TV always under the authority of uncles watching baseball or football—some of us would walk down the road to the little convenience store half a mile away. I loved and loathed this store. Loved because it was the only purveyor of candy and joy to be found. Loathed because it was called Kountry Korner. The store had bars over its windows and dusty shelves of chips and beer. The dimness of the place made me shiver, and I never took much satisfaction out of choosing a Milky Way or shoestring red licorice. Why, oh, why, I wondered, couldn't it have been called Country Corner? There was no need to use *K*s instead of *C*s. I voiced this complaint once, walking there with Crissy, Anh, and cousin Becca, and everyone snickered at me, exchanging glances. Crissy twirled a finger around her ear to say, *Crazy*.

One of my most vivid memories of Fruitport is caught in a photograph: me and Anh in our matching calf-length hooded jackets that Noi had knitted for us out of pink and blue yarn. It is a cold, rainy Easter, the sky like steel behind us. The hem of Anh's maroon dress peeks out from her jacket and she is smiling, having found dozens of Easter eggs in the hunt some of the grown-ups organized. I am so small beside her, six or seven years old, a mere spot of knitted jacket, the hood pulled tight over my head so that only my glasses seem to jut out; my fists are jammed into the patch pockets. My face is stubborn and sad—its usual expression, with an undercurrent of anger at the whole day. I thought of Easter as a mellow form of Christmas, with the Easter Bunny instead of Santa, and baskets of fake grass and chocolate eggs instead of stockings and presents. I didn't care for hard-boiled eggs—no matter how dyed or painted, they were merely eggs, and not my idea of treasure (unless they were well deviled with mustard and paprika). I wanted plastic shells instead, purple and pink opening to reveal M&M's or chocolates wrapped in pastel-colored foil. I believe I found only one or two eggs in that hunt. I was too slow, and my glasses kept getting blurred with drizzle. I could see the grown-ups laughing at me, and I couldn't even blame them. All I wanted was to go home, back to my slice of solitude on the top bunk.

But we kept going back to Rosa's family, of course. Every year the drives grew more silent and tense. My father enjoyed himself about as much as Rosa did at Vietnamese parties. Once in a while, his attention elsewhere, he would miss the highway exit. Rosa would point this out and set him off shouting that he knew how to drive. Had he been permitted to stay in Grand Rapids, he could have met up with his friends at Anazeh Sands for billiards. After a few rounds, which my father would win if he didn't drink too much, they'd end up at someone's house with a deck of cards and a fresh bottle of Hennessy. Rosa knew all too well how my father preferred to spend his weekends, and she wanted to put a stop to it, for he always drank too much and always came home broke. His coats smelled of Winston cigarettes and the metallic tinge of winter air.

For years we went to Fruitport every Thanksgiving and Christmas Eve. We could put it off if Chu Cuong or Chu Dai won a turkey at a bowling tournament, but then we would have to go the day after. No getting around it. I figured it was better to go when the abundance of food hit its peak, when we could be sure to have Grandma's flour tortillas and spicy rich tamales. She made everything from scratch, rolling out each tortilla before dawn. Rosa reheated them directly on the stove's gas burner, over a low flame. With the tips of her fingers she kept flipping the tortillas until they were heated through, then dropped them onto a plate and glossed them up with margarine. I loved that first taste of tortilla: it felt like a flattened pillow between my teeth, an initial bite and chew not unlike that of juice-filled bubblegum.

The tamales encompassed hours of work. Grandma recruited her daughters to soak the corn husks and help her mix together spicy red beef and hand-ground, tender masa. The tamales were prepared and folded by hand in a process as rigorous as making *cha gio,* and steamed until the packages turned tawny. It seemed that the more work it took to make a dish, the better it tasted. We only ate tamales on holidays, and I was aware each time not to take too many. Though I longed to pile my plate with them, quickly unrolling the husks to cram the meat-filled treats into my mouth, I knew that greed was a sin in Rosa's family. If I took three tamales rather than two, a *tía* might glance at my plate and wonder out loud why a little girl like me had eyes bigger than her stomach.

Besides tamales and tortillas, each holiday included a giant turkey that was sometimes cooked for half a day in a pit, a vat of mashed potatoes with gravy boats nearby, Stove Top stuffing, Pillsbury crescent rolls, canned corn soaked in butter, canned string beans mixed with cream of mushroom soup and baked with Durkee fried onions, frijoles, arroz con pollo, pumpkin empanadas, and mashed sweet potatoes covered with mini-marshmallows toasted under the heat of the broiler. One of the *tíos* was married to a white woman who always brought instant pistachio pudding mixed with plenty of Cool Whip and canned pineapple tidbits.

The dessert side of the table held a collection of homemade and store-bought pumpkin pies. I didn't like the texture or the cloying spices in the pumpkin pie, though I would deign to eat a piece if it was smothered in Cool Whip. Mostly I concentrated on the various Jell-Os studded with canned fruit, and the store-bought apple and cherry pies. Cherry was my favorite. I loved fresh cherries above all other summer fruits for their redness, the sweet-tart juice, the danger of their stain. I often begged Rosa to take us cherry-picking in the summer, but she didn't care for cherries as much as blueberries.

I always wished dinner could last longer, for when it was over I had no more purpose in Fruitport. I sometimes got invited to play hide-and-seek or checkers or Monopoly with Anh and cousin Becca. If not, I would retreat to whatever corner or chair I could find and reread the books I had brought. I guarded them, always paranoid that someone would take away my well-worn copy of *Harriet the Spy* or *The Girl with the Silver Eyes*. At Christmas I sat through the gift exchange with little interest. Anh and I always received random pieces of plastic jewelry, and I never had much luck with the "grab bag" of toys the grown-ups passed around to the kids, save for the time I drew out a ten-pack of Carefree gum. After a while, Grandpa would pick up his guitar and serenade the family with beautiful old songs. His voice softened me and made me feel something like homesickness.

It was always late when we finally drove home. In the backseat of our successive cars—the blue Ford Econoline van that my father had carpeted, the maroon Oldsmobile Cutlass Supreme, the tan Mitsubishi Vista—my siblings and I would fall asleep. But once in a while, a wave of alertness washed over me and I would stare out the window, trying to keep my eye trained on a single pine tree as we sped by it. Usually everyone else would be asleep, too, including Rosa in the passenger seat, her head slumped over to one side. My father didn't listen to the radio when he drove, and I could never see his expression in the rearview mirror.

Rosa took offense at how much I resisted Fruitport. To her, it translated to a dislike of her family, simple as that. *You're getting too big for your britches*, she said. "You need to" began many of her sentences. You need to learn more Spanish. You need to play with your cousins. You need to get a better attitude. To which I defended myself once with, "I like tamales and tortillas," and she just stared at me, baffled.

I couldn't explain to her that it wasn't dislike; it was unfamiliarity. Her family didn't know me as I didn't know them. It was too much for me to synthesize white American culture, Mexican-American culture, and my own Vietnamese culture all at the same time. I couldn't explain, either to Rosa or myself, that in wanting to belong everywhere I ended up belonging nowhere at all. "You don't understand" was my standard phrase, a useless catchall to convey what I didn't know how to say. "We're all in this together," Rosa insisted, but it took me years to comprehend what she meant.

I can see the route we always took back home, my father exiting off I-131 at 36th Street toward our neighborhood. Our house lay at the intersection of Sycamore and Florence, and I had nightmares about cars sailing down Sycamore's hill and smashing in our front door. But everything outside was still when my father parked at the curb. On a whim he had bought an old motorboat off the classified pages in the *Grand Rapids Press*. He had talked about spending summer days cruising the small orb of Gun Lake and maybe even Lake Michigan someday, but the motor needed to be repaired and he never did get around to it. Covered with a bright blue tarp, the boat shared the driveway with Rosa's broken-down Toyota. In the summer, Vinh and I might sit in the red vinyl captain's chair, pretending to steer ourselves toward an undiscovered island. Inside the house, Noi had left the lights on for us. Rosa put away some leftovers she had brought back—only once or twice did they contain tamales—and I carried my books down the hall. We were all of us silent at such times, lost in our own thoughts that aimed us in different directions.

13

Stealing Buddha's Dinner

MY SISTER ANH AND I ATTENDED CATHOLIC SCHOOL
for four days in the fall of 1982. St. Joseph's Elementary had old
stone halls that arched into echoes when I and the other third-
graders followed Sister Wendy down to the library. Much to my
disappointment, the younger nuns wore regular clothes. I only
saw black-clad figures and wimples, the fabric stirring slightly, on
the older nuns, the administrator nuns. My frame of reference for
them was *The Sound of Music,* and I kept hoping that these nuns
would break into song. But there were no wayward Marias in
this lot.

Like many immigrant parents, mine believed in education as
a ticket, a necessity, and the only way forward. Rosa believed in
it more than anyone; she'd devoted her whole career to it. But
therein lay one of her many contradictions. She worked in public
schools, and had thrown off the mantle of her Catholic upbringing years ago, but she also believed that St. Joseph's would provide us with better learning and discipline, the latter of which
Anh and I both needed, being prone to temper tantrums.

On that first day of school, before we got our uniforms, Anh wore her favorite dress. It was my favorite, too: a beautiful emerald-green polyester that I called silk, with covered buttons and a sash. At recess—she never had a problem making friends—I watched her from my solitary spot on a wooden jungle gym. She and a group of girls were playing basketball. Her skirt swished as she dribbled the ball, the fabric shining in the sunlight. The next day we had stiff, pleated navy jumpers, plaid blouses, white knee socks. Even though the uniform was scratchy and uncomfortable, I liked that having it meant one less thing to worry about. If everyone dressed the same, I reasoned, everyone would fit in the same. But when I walked into the classroom and all of the students swiveled their heads to stare at me, I remembered that a uniform could not hide my skin or my face. I didn't know then that many Vietnamese were actually Catholics and that some of the refugees in Grand Rapids had been sponsored by local Catholic churches. I didn't know there was any tension between Catholics and Reformed Christians. All such subtleties escaped me; I was still trying to figure out who God was supposed to be.

At lunchtime, everyone ate right at their desks. There was no cafeteria at St. Joseph's and no talking among the students. All morning my gaze had returned to the crucifix pinned above the chalkboard in the center of the room. Sister Wendy informed us that we would take turns saying the lunchtime prayer, and she called on a wispy girl named Lindsay to go first. Lindsay stood up and launched an effortless speech having something to do with gratefulness and Mary, holy mother of God. I copied the other students by lowering my head and pretending to keep my eyes closed, but I was wondering how Mary could be the mother of God. Plus, wasn't she supposed to be a virgin? I knew well the images of Mary with her tranquil expression and blue robe. I pictured her gently chastising God, whom I pictured as Zeus-like, sporting a great flowing beard.

When everyone said "Amen" I repeated it softly. I spent the rest of the lunch hour realizing that I, too, would be called on at some point to say the prayer. There were a little over a dozen of us in the class, which meant that everyone would be praying out loud many times over the course of the year. I wondered if people would simply repeat themselves, and if they did, if they would get in trouble. Were there points for originality? Creativity? Expression? This was public speaking of a terrifying kind, and I knew I could not surmount it. How could I utter words that I had dismissed to Jennifer Vander Wal? I could not give thanks, or bow my head legitimately, or declare *Amen*.

At home I told Rosa about the prayers. She sat down at once to write notes for me and Anh, informing our teachers that we were Buddhist and not Catholic, and therefore not allowed to lead the prayer, ever. The next day Sister Wendy read the note with a somber face. I could see the disapproval in her eyes, and when she put the paper away she glanced at me as if I were some strange, unsightly specimen that she did not know how to treat.

Because St. Joseph's started a full week ahead of public school, I finally got to celebrate my end-of-August birthday during the school year. Birthdays, everyone knew, could only be celebrated appropriately if the birthday kid brought candy for the whole class. Rosa surprised me by buying exactly the kind I wanted: Hershey's miniatures, the variety pack with mini Mr. Goodbars, Krackles, regular Hershey's, and my beloved Special Dark. My classmates regarded me with frank assessment as I handed out the candy. Word had gotten around that I was excused from prayer, which maybe explained why I hadn't yet made any friends. Possibly I was aligned with Satan, someone come to test their faith. Or I was someone to be approached with care, the way missionaries' subjects have to be won over and then broken down. But perhaps they also felt pity, a kind of danger as they unwrapped the chocolates and pressed them into their mouths.

Two days later Rosa pulled Anh and me out of St. Joseph's. She chalked it up to the reality of tuition fees, the chore of keeping our uniforms clean, and having to drive us to and from school every day. The fact was that Ken-O-Sha was an easy three blocks from our house, walkable in any weather. Rosa didn't mention religion, but I knew that was one of the reasons. She had abandoned Catholicism—though a few years later she would reconsider it— and she preferred to keep our household that way, too. Each December my siblings and I would help Rosa unfold the trusty artificial Christmas tree and trim it with the ornaments we had made out of metallic ribbons and Styrofoam balls, thinking only of the gifts we might get to unwrap. In school, we sang "O Come All Ye Faithful" and "Joy to the World" and failed to connect the words to the religion. Rosa once mentioned that her best friend Shirley didn't celebrate Christmas because she was Jewish. When I asked her what that was she said it meant that Jewish people couldn't eat any ham or pork. I figured she was referring to the honey-baked ham we got every holiday. "What about Chu Anh and David and Joseph?" I asked. Every year we sent Christmas cards and gifts to my uncle, Shirley, and their two sons in At- lanta. "Oh, it's just Christmas," my stepmother said. "Nobody has to think about religion until they're grown up."

But of course I did think about it, especially when I moved into my grandmother's room to get away from my sisters. Noi couldn't read my diary, and she didn't mind if I used her closet as my own hideaway. For a while we shared her double bed until Rosa bought me a convertible chair that unfolded into a single bed.

Every evening Noi meditated, sitting on her bedroom floor in front of the family altar and Buddha statue, her back perfectly straight. She didn't stir at all, not even when I barged in, forgetting the hour. When we settled into bed we always slept with our heads facing Buddha as a sign of respect. It wouldn't do to stick our feet out to him. With such a figure looming above me, I thought a lot about reincarnation. I had always vaguely accepted it as the answer to the question of what would happen after death. It made sense to me that one could return and live again. "You get better and better lives," Rosa explained to me, "depending on what kind of person you are in your life now." She talked about reincarnation as something positive, and didn't mention nirvana at all. My father never said anything to correct her.

I took this view of reincarnation on literal terms. I began to guess at the lives I had had. I became convinced that I had once been a sad and lonely blond girl who lived in a cold mansion isolated on a moor in England. I saw myself sitting close to the fireplace in my bedroom, looking out the window at a bleak, gray landscape. No visitors. I had died young there. Then I began to worry about my next life. In terms of being a good person, I had to admit that I wasn't much of one. I often wished Jennifer Vander Wal might fall in mud and spoil her clothes or that Anh and Crissy might receive electric shocks when they tried to read my diary. I harbored hateful feelings toward Rosa and my father— for not letting me join the class trip to Kellogg's cereal factory, for not getting me the backpack I wanted, for yelling at me when they thought I looked at them askance. With such vengeance churning in my mind, I worried I was already doomed to a much

worse life the next time around. I began imagining horrible possibilities that lay in wait for me: I could be a street urchin, a
burglar, a starving farmer. I pictured myself imprisoned and a
chill went through me as if to confirm the truth of the premoni-
tion. I was a criminal in the making. Next life's lifer.

During this time, *2001: A Space Odyssey* was shown on net-
work television and my whole family gathered to watch it. The
movie's eerie images, the stark white mother ship drifting through
all that black space, gripped me with the same anxiety I sometimes felt when I looked up into the night sky. I shivered to think
about life before humans, when, I imagined, the world was a vast
tundra littered with animal carcasses. For months after the movie,
my dreams were filled with visions of an ominous obelisk and a
red glaring button, a voice intoning, *Dave, Dave,* then wavering
into a wail of mournful electronica. I had nightmares of floating
within an amniotic sac. Was this heaven, hell, nirvana? It all
boiled down to the same thing: complete aloneness. I developed
insomnia, a fear of dreaming. I never told anyone about it, but
my grandmother must have guessed, for she sometimes caught
me sitting in the living room by myself at two or three in the
morning, staring out the window at our empty unlit street.

Slowly, Noi brought me back. In the evenings, after dinner,
she served fruit in her room rather than in the kitchen. So we
would sit on her bed or on the floor, a plate of tangerine slices
between us. She didn't mind if I left the television on, and the
glow of her lamps seemed to cast circles of warmth upon us as we
listened to the theme song of *Love Boat* or *The Greatest American
Hero.* On the best winter nights, we ate pomegranates. Anh liked
them as much as I did, and only Noi could referee the fights between us as we each tried to grab a bigger portion. We loved to

watch Noi crack open the fruit, revealing the embedded seeds without bursting even one. An opened pomegranate reminded me of a map—rows of close-fitted houses with red roofs as seen from far above. We helped Noi pick out each kernel, laying them out in piles. Glittering rubies, I thought. We loved to crush them between our teeth, the tart juice staining our mouths.

In the early years in Grand Rapids, my grandmother attended Buddhist temple in a rented house on the south side of town. She was one of the leaders of this makeshift community, and when she stepped out of my father's car on Sunday mornings, wearing her dark *ao dai* and jade pearls, everyone nodded at her with deference. Slowly, she and her friends gathered donations to purchase a vacant church. It sat on a barren plot of land in a section of town that in twenty years would be overrun with strip malls and nail salons. My father helped renovate the church, removing all of the pews to create one open room, refinishing the wood floors to a high gleam, carting in a Buddha statue for the altar. The Buddha stood ten feet tall, a golden presence among masses of flowers and candles.

On Sundays, monks in mustard-colored robes led the prayers and I remember watching Noi join the rows of people already prostrating themselves, all chanting the same chant. I wanted to join, too, but my old shyness kept me hesitating at the door. I worried that I would slip in my socks and fall, causing a scene. In this environment Noi seemed almost unknown to me. She wasn't my grandmother then, but a spiritual being. I backed away and headed to the basement, where women were setting up *cha gio* and sweet bean pastries. My father, who mostly came to temple to socialize with his friends, was already laughing with them in a circle. I felt so out of place—too American, not truly Buddhist—that I never did muster the nerve to enter the prayer room, let alone approach the imposing statue of Buddha.

I decided to practice at home. Here, Buddha was a lot smaller and more familiar to me. He sat on his old shelf, cross-legged, his robe draping in his lap as he held his hands together, palms up. He wore a finely pebbled cap. He had closed eyes and droopy earlobes, which my father said signified his princely origins. It amused Noi to see me taking notes on when to light the candles and incense. She clasped her hands at her chest, rocking them to a repeated singsong chant, every so often stepping forward to tap the little copper bell that lay on the altar. When she bowed and prostrated herself I did the same, trying to pick up the meaning of the movements. Once, when I asked, my father tried to explain the nature of Buddhist prayer to me. "It's not like when the people in church pray to God," he said.

Noi didn't talk about Buddhism; it was simply a part of her, like her silvery knee-length hair she unrolled from its bun every night. I didn't know what kinds of questions I could ask her, and with no formal training in Vietnamese to bolster what I learned at home, my grasp of the language began slipping away. Large chunks of syntax dissolved overnight. It was as though the more English I read and took in from the TV and radio, the less space I had for Vietnamese. By third grade, I could actually feel the words hovering out of reach. I hoped I could learn from Noi by being near her. That if I had an affinity for Buddhism it would happen here. So I watched and followed and jotted notes as she murmured the prayer songs and bowed to the floor. After a while she switched off the light and blew out the candles, and we sat together on the carpet, a royal blue textured in whorls and curli-cues that resembled tidal waves. I tried to make as little sound as possible.

My father said that when Noi meditated she emptied her mind of all thoughts. He claimed that once, in Vietnam, she did it so completely that she began to levitate, her body becoming as weightless as her mind.

As I meditated, I kept my back straight. Noi was strict about that; if she came across one of us kids slouching in front of the TV or at the table she'd give our backs a good hard poke with her finger. After a while, the posture did become habitual, but it didn't help keep my mind from wandering. I thought about ways to empty my mind of all thoughts. *Empty empty empty,* I thought, then chastised myself for thinking it. The more I tried to clear my head, the more cluttered it became. I thought about how Blair Warner on *The Facts of Life* kept her hair so beautifully wavy. I thought about the Rick Springfield record I wanted for my birthday, remembering the tension of the "Jessie's Girl" video—Rick staring at himself in the bathroom mirror, then smashing it with his guitar. *I wanna tell her that I love her but the point is probably moot.* I thought about Noi's room: the blue com-forter, the little TV that gave us *Days of Our Lives* and *Silver Spoons;* the stereo system and stack of Vietnamese opera and folk song cassettes. Over the two windows, one looking out on Flor-ence Street and the other facing the Harrisons' house, vinyl shades hung beneath gauzy white curtains. Behind me, Noi's cul-tivated plants grew and grew.

After a while I couldn't help opening my eyes. Even before I adjusted to the dark I focused on the solid wood credenza that served as the altar. Among the candles, incense, trays of fruit, and vases of gladioli stood black-and-white portraits of my grandfather and uncle—both of them so young and handsome when they died—and Noi's mother. She looked stern and regal, the opaqueness of her *ao dai* matched by her round velvet hat. It had taken my father three years of letters, with American dollars hidden carefully between the pages, to get my grandfather's and uncle's ashes dug up from the burial ground in Saigon and sent to us in Michigan. Noi couldn't bear the thought of abandoning them in Vietnam. At least her parents' ashes were safe in Hanoi with her sisters.

It didn't scare me to think of them resting in the ceramic, floral-patterned urns. My father had always said that their spirits were with us and it seemed a comfort. Not a ghost, but something like memory, a respect for the past. It made sense, too, to offer fruit to the spirits and Buddha. At each mealtime Noi also set aside a plate for the ancestors; she would never let anyone go hungry. Buddha, of course, had more abstemious tastes and didn't need so much. Whatever Noi set on the altar took on a glow of greater resonance, turning an ordinary orange into a radiant globe. In the fall and winter there were apples, pears, tangerines, oranges, and grapefruit. Summer meant plums, peaches, nectarines, and cantaloupe. Bananas were year-round, if they were smooth and unspotted, and sometimes grapes if Noi could get them past Rosa's boycott. The most treasured fruits were mangoes, pomegranates, kiwis, and pineapples. Then, after a period of days that only Noi determined, she would take a piece of fruit from its wrought-iron tray and it would be transformed into human food again.

On Tet, Buddha's birthday, and the anniversary of her husband's and son's deaths, Noi added to the altar an expensive assortment of dried papaya, persimmon, and coconut, tins of cashews and pistachios, and plates heaped with *banh chung* rice cakes, red bean cake pastries, *cha gio,* noodle dishes, and fried shrimp chips. I would imagine my ancestors and relatives descending into the room. They would be more invisible than Wonder Woman's plane outlined in white. They would pick at the fruit, perhaps wishing for the kinds my father talked about having in Vietnam, like the one my father used to hack open on a tree stump with a cleaver. *Stinkyfruit,* he called it, sighing with remembered satisfaction.

While my grandmother meditated for hours, I would sneak away to read in the living room or pilfer whatever sweets I could find in the kitchen. I had taken to hoarding cookies and snack cakes, stashing them away in unused pots that sat in the back of the cabinets. When her meditations were done Noi would open her door to let me know I was free to join her again. She tried to teach me how to knit then, but my practice scarves kept curling into tough, chain-mail-looking shells. Before I went to bed I would ask Noi if it was all right for me to go to sleep. It had become a little ritual between us, and sometimes Noi jokingly answered, *"Khong duoc." It's not okay.* Then I would have to leave the room and return, asking permission until she granted it.

The summer after my third-grade year, I helped Jennifer Vander Wal practice songs for her Sunday school musical. She was only in the chorus, and fiercely resented the girl who had gotten the lead female role of Susie, a vain character who had to learn her lesson that pride goeth before a fall. Still, Jennifer and I practiced every line of *Agapaopolis.* According to the songs, it was a wonderful place—part Candyland, part Disneyland, part heaven.

Jennifer had tapes of the musical from Zondervan, a big Christian bookstore based in Grand Rapids, and we listened to the cheerful melodies for hours. "Agapaopo*lisss*," we sang together. "A place you're wishing that you are!" The star of the show was a gentle young boy who spent the musical leading his friends toward the gates of Agapaopolis. Susie, on the other hand, tossed her hair about and pranced onstage. Jennifer sang Susie's lines with bitterness: "Looking out for good ol' number one, always looking out for good ol' number one. Think you're gonna make it into high society, but you've got a lot to learn about humility!"

One day Jennifer invited her best friends from school, Amy and Rachel, to play with us. They were also in the *Agapaopolis* chorus, and after a practice session—Jennifer loved to be the stand-in for Susie—we played four square in the Vander Wals' driveway. As we bounced a basketball back and forth to each other we compared notes on Clearbrook Christian versus Ken-O-Sha Elementary. At Clearbrook, the girls informed me, everyone liked Dandy Bars and only Jell-O brand pudding cups would do. "We like Swiss Miss," I lied, citing the cheaper brand that my stepmother sometimes bought. Rachel, a tall girl with a close crop of brassy curls, said, "What's your favorite song? *We* like 'There's Always Something There to Remind Me.'"

"I have the *Thriller* record," I bragged, though really it was Anh's, paid for with some of her birthday money. Jennifer had disobeyed her parents when she listened to it, admiring the glow of Michael Jackson's white cuffs on the album cover. Her parents screened every element of media for possible dirtiness; they were suspicious of videos, music with good beats, and anything that might be associated with break dancing. Though my parents had their own worries about dirty music, they couldn't help liking Michael Jackson and his excellent dance moves.

"Wanna go listen to it?" I asked. "We can watch videos, too."

"Can we?" Amy asked, looking to her friends for guidance.

"*I* have records we can listen to," Jennifer said. I knew she meant the Christian ballads her parents collected for her. She always upped the moral ante around her Clearbrook friends. "Anyway, I want to practice *Agapaopolis* again."

"You should see the 'Billie Jean' video," I said to Amy and Rachel. "It's totally awesome."

"We're not supposed to listen to that song," Rachel said primly, sending the basketball in my direction. "It goes against the Lord."

I bounced it back. "How do you know?"

"You just know, just like you know the power of the Lord."

"Not *everybody* knows," Jennifer burst out contemptuously. "*Some* people aren't even baptized and they're going to hell."

I threw the ball with greater force, sending Amy scrambling after it. When she tossed it back I held the ball, pausing the game. I couldn't stop myself from speaking. "If there's a God he can strike me down right now," I said. The girls shrank back and exchanged looks. They waited, perhaps for God to indeed strike me down. For just a moment I waited, too. The cloud puffs in the blue sky shifted a little. A breeze rippled the leaves of the Vander Wals' birch tree, whose bark Jennifer and I had often peeled off to use as paper for our notes. I knew I would have to go home after this, leave Jennifer and her friends to their Kool-Aid and cookies, their dolls and their gossip, their *Agapaopolis*. Later, after Jennifer had had time to think the day over, she would tell me that God is forgiving. That He would give me so many chances to reach out to Him if only I just would.

When the premiere of *Agapaopolis* arrived, I declined Jennifer's invitation to come along to the church and watch. In spite of my curiosity to see the hated girl who played Susie, and to see the production whose songs I had practiced for weeks, I didn't want to sit in the audience with the rest of the Vander Wal family, surrounded by other Christians. I would be too outnumbered, the obvious outsider, nonbeliever, the black-haired possible devil.

Maybe because I was surrounded by so much Christianity, I often regarded Buddha as a stand-in for God. I prayed to him many times for things I wanted: Top 40 albums, new shoes, chocolate cake. I prayed for miracles, too: twenty-twenty vision, a pretty face, big bank accounts for my parents. Whenever God was cited—in the Pledge of Allegiance or on coins—in my mind I substituted the word *Buddha*.

I prayed often during that *Agapaopolis* summer. As I ate ice cream sandwiches from Gas City or filched my favorite blue-hued Otter Pops from the freezer, I would pray for Rosa to realize she should buy me as many sweets as I liked. I prayed for prettier clothes, more money, my own bedroom filled with books and records and tapes. It was a summer of Laura Branigan's "Solitaire," the Police warning us about every breath we took, and David Bowie murmuring "shhhh" to his little China Girl. Crissy was off with her forbidden friends while Anh and I roamed, restless, turning up the radio whenever WGRD played Culture Club and Duran Duran. We played four square, Life, and pickle with Jennifer and our brothers. We watched MTV, wishing we could be as cool as Martha Quinn. All the while I prayed, yet none of my prayers were answered. I woke up with the same blurry vision, the same flat face punctured by the two dimples I hated, the same shortness that made tall people's elbows a constant danger.

So I decided to take it one step further. It was time to tempt Buddha's wrath and see what happened.

One late afternoon when Noi was out watering the garden, I slipped into her room. The day had gotten sticky with humidity, and the brightness of the outdoors made everything inside feel dim. I could tell it was going to be one of those nights when my siblings and I would sleep in the basement to stay cool. I didn't know where everyone was to make the house so empty: Vinh probably playing Transformers somewhere with Jennifer's brother; Anh hanging out at a friend's house; Crissy with her friends, maybe smoking in the parking lot behind Ken-O-Sha; my uncles at their jobs; my father at North American Feather; Rosa working downtown at the Hispanic Institute. For once, I was practically alone in the house.

As I studied the altar, I realized that fruit was all that Buddha had to eat. Except for holidays it was the same thing day in and day out—lunch was dinner, dinner was breakfast. My father had tried to explain that Buddha believed in simplicity and having as few things as possible. So I guessed that he was okay with just fruit—maybe he even preferred it. I couldn't comprehend that. Looking up at Buddha I wanted to ask, *That's all?* I didn't know what it was not to want.

For I could hardly name all the different meals I wished to have. Dinners of sirloin tips and Shake 'n Bake. Beef Stroganoff and shepherd's pie. Jeno's pizzas and thermoses of SpaghettiOs. Great squares of Jell-O bouncing through the air as they did in the commercials; Bundt cakes; chocolate parfaits; rounds of crusty lattice-topped pies. I wanted all the dinners from *Little*

House on the Prairie, all those biscuits and salt pork, grease seeping into the fried potatoes. I wanted every packaged and frozen dinner from the grocery store: Noodle Roni, Hamburger Helper, Hungry Man, Stouffer's, Swanson, and Banquet. All the trays with separate compartments for Salisbury steak, whipped potatoes, and peas. I wanted to take it all, hoard it, hide it away. If I were a spirit, I would fill myself with meals culled from the city around me. People in their pretty houses would sit down to dinners of nothing. They would take their eyes off their plates for just one second and the food would be gone. They would open their refrigerators: empty. Their pantries would be cleaned out. Cupboards bare, the doors swinging open to emphasize the blank space. I would take from restaurants: Brann's, Big Boy, Charley's Crab—all the white American meals I longed to try. If I were a spirit, I would eat more than enough to get me through the night.

In Noi's room the shades were closed against the sun. The air smelled of her favorite sandalwood incense. I sat on the bed for a moment, listening to the quiet of the house. The heat pressed in on me and I shut my eyes, trying to meditate. But I could think of nothing but the altar. The burnished statue of Buddha rose above me. His always closed eyes, his gown of glimmering folds. He was nothing like the fat, happy Buddha statue we had in the basement. That Buddha, dyed a festive red, had an open mouth and eyes squished up in laughter. He sat with one knee raised, showing off his potbelly, not at all resembling this smooth Buddha with his face of radiant calm.

I leaned in close to take in the gazes of my grandfather and great-grandmother. How far these pictures had traveled to come back to us. My father had said the spirits of our ancestors could find us anywhere. In between their photographs two trays held plums, nectarines, and bananas in near-pyramids of offering. An afternoon snack for my ancestors, a dinner for Buddha.

With one fingertip I touched the stem of a plum, whose violet skin always looked dusty. For just a moment, I hovered over it. Then the fruit was lying in the flat of my hand. I looked up at Buddha. His eyes were still closed. Sometimes, when we wanted to scare each other, Anh and I talked about how one day Buddha's eyes would fly open, shooting out beams of light. I waited a minute longer, until I heard the sound of the basement door opening and sliding shut. Then I ran out of the room, pushing the plum into my shorts pocket as I hurried out the front door.

I crossed our yard to the Vander Wals'—Jennifer must have been at vacation Bible school—and shimmied up their plum tree. How many times had Jennifer and I sat up here among the leaves, dreaming up one of our clubs? In the full bloom of summer the leaf-thick limbs took us in and kept us hidden. I settled into my usual spot, where two sturdy branches seemed to create a lounge chair just right for my size. I pulled Buddha's plum from my pocket and examined it as I had when my sister and I were little, marveling at the mystery of fruit. I looked for some answer in its skin but found nothing. The guilt I felt was the same as shame. I knew that this was where the test would end—me in the tree with the stolen plum. My father had said that Buddha had given up all possessions of his royal birth and become enlightened. Buddha never claimed to be a god. He could not be tested. He had no wrath. He granted no miracles or wishes. He asked me to prove nothing.

As I sat in the Vander Wals' tree, Christianity seemed about as real as Agapaopolis. It seemed as distant from my person as blond hair and blue eyes. It also seemed manipulative, what with all that fire and hell. When Jennifer talked about the Lord it was with equal parts love and fear. Noi didn't fear, or even really love, Buddha. She didn't worship him; she gave him her respect. That showed in the way we slept with our heads facing him and in the fruit, incense, and candles set forth each day. When she bowed and chanted she wasn't praying out of fear, or to save herself, or to ask for something good to happen for her. The Christians were God's minions, but Noi was not Buddha's.

I bit into the plum. I was struck, as always, by the contrast of the yellow flesh, limned with the scarlet underside of the skin. I took small bites so as not to waste a drop of juice. Too soon, the fruit was gone and the pit lay in my palm. It was an eye, I realized. A wrinkled, wizened eye. I thought about how the spirits were always watching out for us. They were never too far away. I set the eye on a branch where I could face it, and it me. I sat there for a long time. I heard the sound of Linda Vander Wal's car leaving and then returning, bringing Jennifer back from Bible school. I listened to the car doors slam and the murmur of their voices, the screen door shutting them into their house. The daylight began to glow—that quiescent hour before the beginning of sunset—and I knew it was time to go home. I left the plum's eye in the plum tree. It was gone the next time I climbed up there. I imagined it carried off by the wind, or by my ancestors' spirits, coming to collect the meager offering I had left behind.

14

Ponderosa

WHEN WE LIVED ON FLORENCE STREET, GOING OUT TO dinner meant one of two places: Yen Ching or Chi-Chi's. We never went to Bob Evans, Big Boy, Perkins, Schelde's, or the Ground Round, all of which sounded *bland,* Rosa said. *Too American.* They were the kinds of places that served prime rib specials. My friend Holly knew all about it. In her basement we played waitresses with menus from Bill Knapp's, a white clapboard restaurant with "ye olde English" lettering, faux-wrought-iron sconces, and early-bird and family specials. I'd never been to Bill Knapp's, and trusted Holly's understanding of twice-baked potatoes and smothered chicken. We took imaginary customers' orders and balanced trays of plastic toys that we pretended were salads and steaks.

When it came to American restaurants, my parents seemed to approve only of the low and the high—fast food and expensive seafood. One to get, the other to dream about. When we drove past Charley's Crab downtown, its façade of broad windows lit up with a giant neon crab, all of it thoroughly out of reach, my father would murmur an *ahhh* sound. Good seafood was a link to Vietnam for my father, uncles, and Noi. In the Midwest, it was also a luxury.

Yen Ching still sits near Woodland Mall on 28th Street, with the same yellow and red exterior and pagoda-ish roof. Its sign bears the standard "Asian" font—choppy strokes to evoke kung fu and calligraphy—and the menu has chop suey for non-Asians to order. Back then it was a closed-off place, part of the separate world I kept from my friends at school. It was also like the feeling of having a secret lover. Yen Ching had a dark interior, glamorous red-fringed lanterns, silkscreen artwork on the walls, and Confucian calendars printed on the place mats. If you were born in the Year of the Tiger, the place mats said, you were bold and ferocious. Tigers made excellent matadors and race car drivers. Beethoven, Eisenhower, and Marilyn Monroe—all tigers!

If we were lucky we got to sit at one of the round tables with a lazy Susan in the middle, better for sharing the dishes of shrimp, chicken with snow peas, cashew chicken, sweet and sour pork, and Mongolian beef, plus egg drop soup and egg rolls for all. Crissy, who to this day will not touch a bite of seafood, could eat the entire platter of beef by herself, barely letting me snatch a spoonful of the sweet, soft meat and the strings of caramelized onion. I always sat next to Noi, who snapped up choice bits of pineapple, cashew, and chicken with her chopsticks and deposited them on my plate. She was comfortable in a place like Yen Ching, where the rice arrived perfectly steamed and the menu listed more than a dozen versions of shrimp and fish. She ate the way Vietnamese ate, with the rice bowl close to her mouth. The slurp of soup and suck of shrimp shells—these were the sounds of a good meal. I didn't think anything wrong with it until I noticed Crissy wrinkling up her whole face in disgust.

Crissy preferred Chi-Chi's and so did Rosa, though she'd grown up eating real tortillas handmade before dawn, frijoles simmered for hours, and pico de gallo spiked with fresh cilantro and bracing chilies. I liked Chi-Chi's for the buoyed feeling of family togetherness I felt whenever we went there, all of us trying to consume as much as possible of the free chips and salsa. Rosa lingered over the menu, pronouncing all the words emphatically. "Do you want a tosTAAHHdah," Anh and I would mimic her, dissolving into giggles. "How about a FLOOUUta?" We had to choose from the dreaded children's menu, limited as all such menus were, with its meager assortment of tacos and burritos.

My father always liked the steak and chicken fajitas, which arrived sizzling in a cast-iron pan. The thin, wafery tortillas came from a plastic warmer made to look like a terra-cotta crock. Noi didn't care for Chi-Chi's, though she'd take a few bites of the dry Mexican rice. But surely she, too, was charmed by the restaurant's dimmed lighting, faux-stucco walls, and potted plants with giant fronds. The candles glowing in resin holders on every table made the place seem downright fancy. The waitresses, wearing big Mexican dresses that ruffled off the shoulder and down to the ankle in dramatic flounces, swooshed around us with their trays. I sometimes wished Rosa could give up her job at the Hispanic Institute and work at Chi-Chi's instead.

It was an arrangement that worked for a while—Yen Ching, Chi-Chi's, fast food. At home, Noi did most of the cooking and Rosa chipped in with *sopa* and tacos. *We can be a nice family*, I wrote in my diary, an uncertain declaration.

If I had to pinpoint a time, a year of change, I would begin in 1984. The year of *Like a Virgin* and *Purple Rain*, Crissy's first boyfriends, Brownie troop, *The Karate Kid*, and a new mini-air-hockey table purchased for our basement. And my father and Rosa, quarreling, expanding the fissures in the plate tectonics of our household.

That summer, the Kentwood Public Library gave out free lunch vouchers to Denny's anytime a kid checked out a book. The meal options were spaghetti, hot dog, hamburger, grilled cheese sandwich. To Rosa the vouchers were like gold. She never took us to the library, or out to lunch, as often as she did that summer. In fact she was around a lot more than usual, though it took me a while to notice the sighing, tired look on her face.

I thought I would never get tired of Denny's, but after only a few weeks I grew irritated at the watery spaghetti noodles and unwavering menu. Rosa kept us going there anyway, determined not to waste free food. She was keeping a closer eye on us now, scaring Crissy's boyfriend Kenny away from the house and monitoring what we watched on TV. She was often around when my father wasn't. At night when he came home—from work or from seeing his friends—we all seemed to scatter. It was a small house, but there was a lot of different music playing in different rooms. My uncles liked the *Born in the USA* album. Crissy was getting into Ratt, Van Halen, the Violent Femmes, and anything with a punk edge, which meant the rest of us kids were getting into it, too. At the same time, Anh danced on her own to "The Glamorous Life," aspiring to be Sheila E. I liked dopey ballads and narrative videos on MTV: "Time after Time," "Love Is a Battlefield,"

"Beat It," and "Legs." I liked how Cyndi Lauper stared forlornly out a train window and how Pat Benatar swung her shoulders at a pimp in a bar. I pretended to dance my way down a street, breaking up a knife fight; then, under the supervision of ZZ Top and their trio of women, I would be transformed from a demure girl into a vampy coquette with stiletto heels.

Rosa was singing different songs: "You Don't Bring Me Flowers Anymore," and Donna Summer's "She Works Hard for the Money." My father, perhaps paying attention, perhaps not, didn't listen to any music at all.

For he and Rosa were, increasingly, at odds. It seemed that the more she talked about "outreach" and "community" at the Hispanic Institute, the more my father grumbled about North American Feather. He went alone to the weekend Vietnamese parties and spent all of his spare time at Anazeh Sands or some friend's dining room table, smoking, drinking, and playing cards. If he happened to win, then he would be in a good mood, but those days were few and far between. At home, he and Rosa glared at each other, fighting about the parties, the drinking, and most of all, the money he kept pulling from their account to finance his nights out.

In the top drawer of Noi's credenza, I hoarded the tens and twenties I had collected over a year of Christmas, Tet, and my birthday. I used to love opening that drawer just before bedtime, to see all that money fanned out before me. It meant more than candy from Gas City and treats from the ice cream truck. It might mean the new shirt and pair of shoes that Rosa wouldn't be willing to buy; it might mean so many books, if only I could persuade someone to take me to Schuler's Bookstore. Then one night I opened that top drawer and found only empty space.

Noi, who consoled me with oranges and tart raspberry-shaped candies, confronted my father the next day. He flew into a rage, which meant he'd lost all the money gambling. "That's *my* money!" he shouted. "I give you everything," he added, wheeling about to point a finger at me. I looked down at my feet, feeling the truth and guilt of his statement, thinking of all he had given me. Life. Flight. Clothes and candy and pop and potato chips. A better existence. Silently I promised him never to say a word about the money again. In the future, I would slip my holiday and birthday bills into pages of my books, feeling so shameful and stealthy that I often forgot the hiding spots. Months later a twenty might fall out onto my lap. My cheeks would burn, remembering my father's words.

We went on like this. The Denny's coupons ran out. I kept playing waitress with my friend Holly. Every once in a while my family would eat at Yen Ching or Chi-Chi's, go home in good spirits, then fall back into moodiness. We said *shut up, be quiet, cállate la boca*. We tread lightly around my father.

Rosa tried to rein him in with house projects. She figured that if he was busy working he wouldn't have time to go out partying so much. She pointed out what a great job he had done when we first moved into the house on Florence. He had stripped away the silver disco wallpaper in the kitchen and painted the cabinets white. In the basement he laid new carpet—a pattern of burnt golds and reds they had picked out together at the Carpet Factory. They had torn down the black padded bar area and covered the walls with sensible wood paneling. The basement was part family area, part bachelor pad. On one side my uncles kept their stereo equipment, crates of albums and cassettes, and over-sized zebra-striped pillows. They indulged in black leather Eames loungers from the Herman Miller store. On the other side of the basement, board games were scattered across the floor with *Highlights* magazines, Magic Markers, knock-off Barbie dolls, and volumes from Rosa's impulse purchase: a complete set of the 1979 *World Book Encyclopedia*.

My father had a natural talent with carpentry, Rosa kept saying. She encouraged him to install an aboveground pool in the backyard. It was the only one in the neighborhood, though the old couple on Sienna Street had a gorgeous in-ground number protected by a fence. They invited only the Vander Wals once or twice a season. From our bloated tub we could hear their polite splashes, and shouted to drown them out, swimming in circles to create a whirlpool. Rosa was making a little more money now, and my father, too, at North American Feather. So they decided they could afford an addition to the house, to create a new dining room on the first floor and family room in the basement. My father did all of the interior work, from the drywall to the tile. He had great plans for a deck off the dining room, and installed a windowed door, painted a summery shade of persimmon. Rosa scoured the furniture sales and bought a mahogany dining table with brass piping along the legs. The matching chairs had seat cushions upholstered in a leaf-green velvety fabric. The set had been done in a style that Rosa called "contemporary," which seemed to describe every Vietnamese home I'd seen: puffy leather couches, brass lamps, and glass-topped tables accompanied the requisite lacquer wall hangings depicting fishermen and farmers in mother-of-pearl designs.

In our new dining room Noi arranged tall potted plants

around the windows. When it would get too hot in the summer she would sometimes sleep on the cold green tile, laying only a sheet between her body and the floor. I tried it once, to keep her company, but couldn't last longer than twenty minutes. She laughed to see my discomfort. In Vietnam she had slept on solid wood bedsteads—no mattress. My parents, meanwhile, picked out a new waterbed for themselves. At the Waterbed Gallery they flopped right down on the test models, their bodies swaying with the suppressed waves beneath them. There was almost nothing Rosa would say no to, it seemed, in order to keep my father at home.

The addition to the house was complete by the fall of 1985, when Rosa announced that we would be getting a new brother. A foster brother, she explained, practically fresh off the boat from a refugee camp. He'd been staying with a Vietnamese widower in Kentwood, but Rosa (who knew everyone's business) felt that he needed a real family to get him acclimated. *Ours,* she emphasized, a kind of rallying demand for unity. The news sent me into a tailspin. I wondered how I was going to explain this to my friends at school. As it was, no one else lived with their grandmother and uncles; no one else had a stepsister and a half-brother.

Huynh was sixteen years old. He had fled Vietnam on a fishing boat while his mother and younger siblings remained in Saigon. For much of the past year he'd been stuck in a refugee camp in the Philippines, waiting for a sponsor. Now he was sleeping on our living room couch or the basement couch or anywhere my parents could find a place. Rosa worked him into our dish-washing rotation, assigned him to rake leaves, and enrolled him in bilingual ed classes at a big public high school downtown. He was one of us and yet he wasn't. Everything about him was strange to me: his accent, his tentative demeanor, his story of riding the sea with a small band of refugees, hoping not to capsize or be caught by pirates. He didn't talk much, and Rosa warned us not to bother him with questions.

Vinh, the sweet, easy one of us kids, befriended him instantly. Together they watched Saturday cartoons and after-school cartoons, and raced Hot Wheels. My sisters and I lurked, not knowing what to say to Huynh. I was ashamed of my inward thoughts: that I was glad I didn't have the heavy accent he had to work against; that I resented his presence, reminding me as it did of my own refugee status. I had almost convinced myself I wasn't an immigrant at all. Every time Tom Petty sang *You don't have to live like a refugee* on the radio, I looked for a different station. I wasn't exactly sure what the song was about, but it seemed taunting; in my mind, the word *refugee* had become embarrassing, synonymous with *foreign, weird.*

Huynh didn't stay long enough with us for me to face my shame. He was miserable in Grand Rapids (that part I could understand), where kids at school openly laughed at him and mocked his speech, and life on Florence Street was no great improvement from life with the widower who had sponsored him in the first place. One winter afternoon, about a month after he had come to live with us, he ran away, his footprints plain in the backyard of snow. He came back later, only to leave again. Back and forth he went, from us to the widower, until finally my parents let him go.

But Rosa was determined to make things work. In early

1986, when I was eleven and a half, she announced the arrival of Phuong and Vu, brothers from Saigon. They had been languishing in a refugee camp, Rosa said, after a harrowing boat ride from Saigon similar to Huynh's. It was our duty to welcome our new brothers, she reminded us. "It's time to give back," she said, looking straight at me.

Phuong was about Crissy's age and Vu was about my age, though I couldn't be sure, because their paperwork had been changed so they could get a few more years of public schooling. They were quiet, shy, and rode a school bus together downtown. Vinh befriended Vu as he had Huynh. Phuong worked with my father on weekends, fixing up the house. Crissy, Anh, and I mostly stayed on the sidelines. We had been used to being the girls, so outnumbering Vinh that we made him one of us, even dressing him up as a doll sometimes. It was a disconcerting shift in power with two more boys in the house, and we girls didn't know what to make of it. My father and Rosa carried on as they always had, my father brooding, Rosa cheerful and pragmatic, telling our foster brothers to call her *Mom*.

In the spring of 1986 my father stopped working at North American Feather. We all said he had quit, but I had to wonder if he'd been fired for showing up late too many times and getting into fights with his coworkers. We went out to Yen Ching on the day my father and Rosa decided that he would become an independent contractor. He would be good at it, for didn't everyone who stepped into the house admire the precision of his tiling, the careful grout, the shelves in the basement? He had an eye for clean lines and he had learned in Vietnam the basics of plumbing and electrical wiring. A fresh start, Rosa emphasized, was what he needed—what we all needed.

Which led, later that year, to the surprise announcement that we would be moving. I had seen my father and Rosa glancing at the real estate section of the *Press* but I wasn't prepared to hear that they'd actually bought a new house. It was located half an hour away, in Ada, a suburb east of town, notable for being the headquarters of Amway.

Rosa said we needed the extra space. She touted Ada as being "in the country," which failed to thrill us kids. She had other reasons for wanting to move: there were too many kids now in our neighborhood, and the summer days of chasing after the ice cream man had given way to real adolescence for Anh and Crissy; the boys who lived up the block were increasing threats to their virginity. There was motivation, too, in getting my father away from southeast Grand Rapids and the heart of the Vietnamese community. Not that Rosa said any of this. I discerned the truth in her voice, in the way my sisters whispered on the phone to boys, and in the way my father would swing his car up to the curb far too late at night. Outside, weeds sprouted in the driveway cracks. The Vander Wals, too, had been trying to move for a while, a brown Century 21 sign stuck in their lawn for months.

My father never did get around to building the much-promised deck off the dining room at the Florence Street house. When he removed the doorknob and stuffed up the space with paper towels—afraid that one of us kids would open the door and fall to the ground below—we knew the deck would never happen. Though he talked about how great it would be to sit out there in the evenings and barbecue shrimp, when we moved to Ada the space remained, an unfulfilled promise.

Rosa called the new house in Ada a dream house, but I didn't know whose dream she was talking about. The only thing I liked about it was the driveway: it tunneled nearly a quarter of a mile through a canopy of oak and willow trees and crossed over a tiny creek that meandered by a small, scummy pond. I liked being set back from the road and hidden from view. The house itself was a dark-brown A-frame with a short wing protruding on either side. It looked like a sad imitation of a country cottage I had seen in one of the *Better Homes and Gardens* magazines Rosa sometimes bought. My parents praised the grove of woods that grew around the house, and Rosa boasted that the house stood on almost four acres. I didn't care about acres. I didn't like country houses any more than I liked the Kountry Korner on a dusty, lonely road in Fruitport. Inside, brown shag carpet spread out in every direction, and the dining room had been decorated with forestry wall coverings. Rosa saved her trump card for last: an enclosed swimming pool that jutted out the back of the house. It was an echoey room with a high, unfinished ceiling, more eerie than inviting. Rosa kept saying, "You can go swimming in the winter. Won't your friends be jealous?" But I had a feeling that we wouldn't be doing much of that, since my parents were always fretting about the cost of heat and electricity. "Every time you plug in that curling iron," my father was fond of warning us girls, "it costs me five dollars."

My parents had been able to buy the house only because it had been in foreclosure, and even then they'd had to use up all their savings and empty our college funds. It was news to me that such funds had ever existed. Chu Cuong and Chu Dai, spurred by the move, finally got their own apartment. They took with them their Eames chairs and zebra-patterned pillows, their tapes and ice cream and cans of pop. Just like that, after living with them my whole life and sitting near their room to hear their music, they were gone.

Moving to Ada didn't stop my father from going out at night and returning red-faced with drink. He simply drove farther to get to the parties. With no steady factory job to clock in and out of, he stayed out later, the headlights of his truck searching their way down the driveway long past midnight. He seemed to build his contractor business around his social life, taking leisurely months to tile a friend's kitchen or drywall a basement. Rosa retreated into her work at the Hispanic Institute. She sat on the board of several nonprofit organizations and spent evenings at committee meetings for literacy groups, La Raza, and United Way. She and my father almost bypassed each other, save for their late-night arguments that often sounded like muffled barks. In the morning I would sometimes find my father sleeping on the leather sofa in the living room.

All the vaunted house space didn't bring the family together. If anything, it gave us room to avoid each other more. Vinh and Vu might play fetch with our Lhasa apso, Lady (Mimi's successor), and I'd walk past them to explore the little creek and pace up and down the driveway. Anh and Crissy squirreled themselves away to read *Cosmo*, talk on the phone, and try out new hairdos. Phuong often went to work with my father, or took extra vocational skills classes on his own. Somehow he and Vu fit right into our fractured family, becoming a part of the silent chaos. Outside, Noi put the gardens to order. I wished many times that I could be like her, so absorbed in work, blessedly solitary, unanxious about the rest of the world.

It was the spring of 1987 and I was finishing seventh grade at the City School, where Crissy and Anh had preceded me. It should have been my kind of place, a charter school for "gifted and talented" students. No sports or PE here, just academics, arts, and lots of kids who worried about their grades. But I didn't fit in even here. I was disorganized, unkempt, while everyone else carried hole punchers in their backpacks and big three-ring binders with at least twenty-five different color-coded tabs. Each semester all of the GPAs above 3.5 were printed out and posted on the walls: a long dot-matrix list on green and white paper, plain facts and fate. Seventh grade was still seventh grade—awkward, self-conscious—and even in the "smart school" cliques formed around the pretty ones.

Because my parents could not control each other they tried to control their kids. Crissy and Anh got the brunt of it, for they were the ones who wanted to attend the forbidden school dances and go out with friends on weekends. Any mention of boys was strictly off-limits. So Anh and Crissy did what they had to do: they sneaked out. They hid makeup and cigarettes in their purses. They used girlfriends as alibis in order to meet boys at Woodland Mall. When I heard them revving up Led Zeppelin or the Steve Miller Band while they curled their hair and applied fresh coats of mascara, I knew they were going someplace that I could not go. They pushed me out of the bathroom, spraying so much Aqua Net and White Rain that a film formed over the mirror.

It was that summer that my father discovered Ponderosa.

The steakhouse chain trumpeted low prices and the longest all-you-can-eat buffet in town: basins of macaroni and cheese, three-bean casserole, minestrone soup, pasta salad, mashed potatoes, stuffing, biscuits and gravy, Jell-O parfait, and all manner of

deep-fried shrimp, chicken, and onions. The ribeye steaks—
$7.99, including a baked potato and the full buffet—bore cross-
hatched grill marks and little plastic flags, stuck into them like
yard signs, that declared "medium well." That's how Rosa said
we should always order steak. It was as tender as dough, with a
smoky flavor that made me imagine great orange flames licking
at the underside of the meat. The baked potatoes, wrapped in
foil, had a bit of frothy innard peeping out, tinted yellow from
the melting pat of margarine, and sprinkled with dried parsley.
And after all that came the sundae bar, with a self-serve machine
that pushed out soft vanilla or chocolate flavors that began melting as soon as they touched the bowls. There were tubs of hot
fudge, caramel, and strawberry sauce, chocolate and rainbow-
colored sprinkles, mini chocolate chips, nuts, and maraschino
cherries.

Rosa's previous complaints about American food went out
the window. We went to Ponderosa almost once a week, telling
ourselves that we were saving money by eating all we could hold.
I could leave plates of uneaten food without attracting a single
lecture about the starving children in Vietnam. We traveled to
and from Ponderosa as a family. There could be no fighting over
the last piece of fried chicken when the buffet held plenty for all.
Here, we could find a common ground.

But of course it couldn't last. We grew tired of the same rib-
eyes and baked potatoes. We grew tired of looking at each other.
I began to realize that the steak wasn't so much tender as it was
fatty. And not so much char-grilled as it was artificially flavored.
I began to eye the uniform grill marks with suspicion, and to
chew slowly to discern the real flavor of beef. It occurred to me
that it tasted nothing like the beef Noi sliced and stir-fried,

dipped into *pho,* and seared with garlic. I noticed that the brick-colored floor of Ponderosa looked like the floor at Burger King. I grew impatient when dishes on the buffet took a long time to get refilled. The restaurant started to feel like what it was: a cafeteria. Even the soft-serve ice cream didn't taste good anymore. It was as unsatisfying as frozen yogurt, melting into inedible liquid, stained with fuchsia maraschino juice.

There was no one dinner that turned the tide. At some point, the savory bite of steak turned into a gristly lump. Margarine congealed on a collapsed, half-eaten baked potato, and the thought of my father taking home the leftovers and heating it all up in the microwave the next day filled me with sadness. Our visits to Ponderosa tapered off, until one day I realized we hadn't gone in weeks. I couldn't remember, either, when we had stopped eating at Yen Ching and Chi-Chi's. Around this time, I worked up the nerve to refuse traveling to Fruitport. I simply said, "I don't want to go." To my surprise, Rosa didn't protest, and I walked away feeling off-kilter. Something had altered in my family and I didn't know how to identify it. The definition of family, of what it meant and determined, had been shifted—by my father, the arrival of my new foster brothers, and now by me.

It wasn't until after we stopped going to Ponderosa that the name of the restaurant struck me, a signpost instruction in my mind: Ponder Rosa.

In the mornings I would make my stepmother a cup of coffee with one spoonful of instant Nescafé, one spoonful of sugar, and one spoonful of Coffee-mate creamer. She was always rushing, late for work, a hundred meetings filling up her day planner. Her papers and files spilled across the dining room table. She would come home from work so exhausted she hardly had the energy, in the winter, to take off her boots, so I would do it for her. I remember the cold, stacked heel of the boots, which were a wine-colored leather, dirty with slush. At these times she seemed sadder than I ever imagined her being; great heaving sighs ran the length of her whole body, and she would collapse into bed. My father would be out somewhere—"working," we said.

I pondered Rosa when I found worn paperbacks titled *Codependency No More* and *When You Love Too Much* stuffed into a junk drawer in the front hall credenza. My father stayed away more and more that year, avoiding Anh and Crissy's rebellions and their teased hair that literally spiraled out of control. Rosa took on a quiet, acquiescent mood that made me want to tiptoe around her.

She had thought that isolating us in Ada would keep us safe and keep us together. But it left us all, I think, feeling lonely. Vinh could play with Vu, who was tolerant and up for all games, but I missed riding a bicycle over the hills of Sienna and Pinewood Streets. I even missed Jennifer Vander Wal's companionship. In our new house, the loft Anh and I shared was narrow and had no door: the staircase from the living room led directly to our room. At night the slanted walls of the A-frame seemed to close down on me. The single window looked out onto the property beyond ours, which belonged to a storage warehouse. Someone had left an abandoned cement stoop—three steps and a wrought-iron railing—in the field and every time I looked out the bedroom window I saw it. "The stairway to nowhere," I joked to Anh, but she just rolled her eyes. I roamed the house, looking for something to do.

The next summer, storms squalled over the yard, rippling the murky pond and bending the willow trees toward the ground. Rosa would wring her hands over the dwindling branches. In the afternoons Vinh and I would walk slowly down the driveway to fetch the mail. Dragonflies hovered over the stagnant pond where Crissy swam once on a dare. She was so often away now, hanging with friends who had their own cars, or working her part-time job at an animal shelter. Noi spent afternoons with her soap operas and knitting. I never knew how she could stand all that cotton, wool, and acrylic, smothering. But her room, as it had on Florence Street, provided a well of solace with its bright blue carpeting, Buddha altar, and shrine to the ancestors. She had a collection of plants near the sliding glass door that led to the backyard, and a new blue La-Z-Boy chair that faced the television. Every day I joined her to watch shows like *Santa Barbara, The Price Is Right,* and *Sale of the Century.* The room was large enough for me to practice cartwheels while Noi sat cross-legged before one of her giant puzzles, pieced together on the same sheet of cardboard my father had found for her years ago. In the evenings, the pine walls glowed in the lamplight when Noi sat down to peel a piece of fruit and snack on a handful of Cheerios. If she had a leftover ear of corn on the cob she'd break off whole rows still intact. She would loosen the knot of her hair, letting it shine to the floor.

One hot morning Rosa drove Anh, Vinh, Vu, and me an hour and a half north to the town of Baldwin. She wanted to see the Shrine of the Pines, which turned out to be a log cabin that someone had built by hand in the late 1800s. Everything in it was made of white pine—rocking chairs, gun racks, a table carved out of an enormous stump, all intricately detailed by one pine-obsessed guy. There wasn't much else going on in that town. Rosa saved the tourist brochures and mulled over magnets in the gift shop. She looked at everything, lingering. On the way back home we stopped at White Cloud State Park to eat the lunch we had brought—sandwiches, chips, and pop—at a picnic table near a trailhead. I remember how the wind kicked up in the trees above us, making a rushing sound among the leaves. Rosa got up and walked into the distance to a water fountain near the parking lot. For one brief moment I had a crazy thought that she was going to get in the car and zoom off without us. But she came back, moving slowly as if each step cost her something. She took her time driving home, taking slow roads while the rest of us nodded off to sleep. Still we made it back long before my father did from wherever he had been with his friends.

The next week, she took us blueberry picking. It was something she liked to do every year, dragging us with her to one of the many "U Pick It" blueberry farms near Lake Michigan. I enjoyed the task at first; there was something satisfying about finding the juiciest, ripest-looking berries and plucking them free. Their stem ends resembled flattened crowns. I ate a few while I picked, but not too many, remembering what Rosa said about pesticides giving people cancer. After an hour or so I grew weary, the hot sun in my face. That's when Rosa would remind us of the full summer days she spent picking berries when she was a child. Grandma and Grandpa did this all their lives, she admonished us. When at last Rosa deemed that we had picked enough, we carried our buckets to the weigh station. It drove Anh nuts that we always picked more than Rosa was willing to buy. We brought home nine or ten pounds, half of which would go into the freezer, to supply us with blueberries through the fall and winter. We had learned to love the cold crunch of frozen blueberries eaten straight from the Ziploc bag.

That afternoon, back from the blueberry farm, Rosa dumped a load of berries into a pot on the stove. I asked her what she was doing. I could see the lines in her face and around her mouth, the way she kept all of her attention on the cooking. She said, "I'm making pies today." I was afraid of her voice, calm as a river covering a bed of razors. Outside, Anh was baking in the sun with her coating of Bain de Soleil. Vinh and Vu were tidying up the yard from the last summer storm. I could hear them competing in a match to see who could hit a distant tree with a rock.

"Do you need any help?" I asked Rosa.

She said she didn't. She pulled out four ready-made graham cracker crusts and lined them up on the counter.

I used to wish Rosa would make lattice-top pies and cool them on a windowsill, as I had seen in comic strips. I loved the construction of a pie, the swell of pastry cradling fruit. It was easy to bake a cake from a Duncan Hines mix, but no one in our household had ever attempted an actual pie. So it was bizarre to see Rosa hovering over the pot of blueberries, mixing in cornstarch and a stream of sugar. She stirred the mixture hard, the curls of her hair trembling. Then she scooped the whole mess into the pie shells, evening the tops with the back of the spoon. She turned the oven on and without waiting for it to preheat she stuck two of the pies in, the tin pans crackling under her hands, and slammed the door shut.

Later, all four pies sat cooling on the kitchen counter. They were heavy and purpled around the edges, and a tough skin had formed over the tops. I asked Rosa if I could have a piece and she told me to help myself. I poured a glass of milk and chose what appeared to be the most pie-looking pie. The blueberry juices had mostly cooked away so that the filling looked as viscous as bean paste. The graham cracker crust had baked into a durable shell that I had to break with the knife point. I overturned a gloppy portion onto my paper plate and took a bite. It was a mouthful of syrup, sweeter than the Hostess pies whose half-moon shapes were finished with a sugar glaze, the original blue-berryness cooked out. I could not get past two bites and neither could anyone else, for by the middle of the next day not even half of one pie was gone. The day after that temperatures soared into the nineties but the pies remained, attracting a bevy of flies. No one touched them. No one dared to move them.

My father got home earlier than usual, but he and my mother walked past each other. As night fell, my father sat outside by himself. He was drinking cognac, probably. My mother glanced at him out the window for a moment, then went to bed.

It was too hot to sleep and we had no air conditioning. Anh and I decided to try the living room. We set fans against the open sliding glass door and camped out on sofa cushions. After a while she drifted off, but I stayed awake, flipping my pillow over to find a cool spot. Finally I got up and went to the kitchen. The orange fluorescence of a new construction site next door reached through the kitchen windows and made the pies look lurid and ghastly. I sat at the counter for a while, pondering Rosa in these pies. When Vinh appeared, also unable to sleep, we decided to throw out the pies, crushing them into a brown paper bag. We pushed that bag into a plastic sack and left it in the corner. Then we searched for something to eat. Anything but pie. We dug up old rolls, pickles, and mustard; a two-liter bottle of Sprite. We sawed away at the block of government cheese. We ate silently, filling up the hunger, eating instead of talking so as not to wake up our house.

The following summer, I was fourteen. Another hot day, another announcement from Rosa: "Your dad and I got divorced." Her voice quieter than I had ever heard it. She hugged each of us, and I remember the way my wrists dangled at her backside when she held me. Then she took us all out to Sizzler, where none of us had been before. It was the middle of the afternoon and the restaurant was empty. It showcased a buffet, smaller and grimier than Ponderosa's, but we just ordered french fries and chicken fingers and pop. A few solitary diners roved around the buffet, scraping the salad bowl with tongs.

We didn't have much to say. We all knew a few kids with divorced parents, but they made up a small fraction of our classes. I tried to imagine my father taking a sad bachelor apartment in some complex off the expressway. Would we have scheduled visits with him, see him only on weekends?

I sipped away at the melted ice in my Sprite while Vinh and Vu started running their fingers through the smear of ketchup on their plates. I didn't like the taste or smell of ketchup, but I leaned over anyway to help them draw zigzags and swirls. We opened packets of sugar and Sweet 'N Low and created starry knolls all over the table. After a while Anh gave in and joined us. Rosa didn't stop us, or lecture us to think about the people whose job it was to clean up. She simply let us make a mess in the Sizzler, and we stayed there long past the end of our meal.

But no one mentioned the divorce again. My father, in fact,

never once spoke the word. I don't recall him ever moving out of the house. He and Rosa went on living the way they always had, except my father slept on the worn black leather sectional in the living room. After a few months we almost forgot that they were ever divorced at all. It was another one of their unspoken arrangements. We all bowed to it, skirting it, never once asking a direct question about their relationship, their lives, our lives.

Rosa had moved us to Ada to keep us isolated and safe and, I suppose, she succeeded. My parents endured each other as they endured the tornado warnings that pulsed over Michigan every spring and summer. They waited it out. I became, in hindsight, the spy I had once longed to be, skulking around, trying to eavesdrop.

When I visit my parents now and drive through Grand Rapids, I sometimes look for the false-front shape of the Ponderosa restaurant and its hokey Old West signage. It used to be welcoming, an entrance into a no-holds-barred, up-for-grabs kind of territory. Now I see the myth of endlessness. The bottomless bowl of soup is never bottomless; the limitless trips to the salad bar always met a limit. Eventually, the longest, biggest buffet in Grand Rapids must end. *All you can eat* is a lure and a dare. "They'll see how much I can eat," my father promised once, speaking to our family generally. He said he'd run the restaurant bankrupt if he had to. We ate like marathoners, as if we could truly fill ourselves up, as if we wouldn't start all over again the next day, hungry.

In this All-American City rife with new Old Country Buffets, China Buffets, and India Buffets, I look back on Ponderosa, and the years that unraveled after it, and I mourn the false hope of all those vats of food. How slick they became, how glutinous the portions, cold on my cold plate. So much emptiness in so much possibility. And out in Ada, the promise of open space became the curse of growing up, of watching my parents morph and struggle while I said nothing but remembered everything. Then I could no longer claim to be a child. That long-ago day at the Sizzler, I had looked at the lit-up dinner menu and realized: Kids Menu, 12 and under. I had spent years wishing to pass that mark and it had happened without my even noticing.

15

Mooncakes

WHEN THE LETTER FROM MY MOTHER ARRIVED, I WAS writing a report on waterfalls of the world for my fifth-grade segment on geography. Angel, Ribbon, and Victoria falls were my primary interests, though I could never see angels or ribbons in the encyclopedia photos. I spent hours trying to draw them, to generate a mist that resembled a halo or a flutter of wings. The letter came from a women's housing center in Swarthmore, Pennsylvania. While I had been playing four square at recess and lingering over fruit roll-ups and Capri Suns at lunch, my mother had boarded planes in Saigon, Singapore, and Los Angeles. She had touched down in America without so much as a glimmer of recognition from me.

I never read or saw the actual letter, which must have passed quietly through my father's and stepmother's hands. If it was a shock they didn't show it. They presented me and Anh with the news almost casually. Just the facts. Guess what happened?

My father and Rosa told us that we could write her back. To me, this was a good, concrete thing we could do to offset the unspoken questions in our minds. *How did she get here? Why*

Pennsylvania? Is she going to come see us? Where will she live? We set about fashioning greeting cards out of construction paper. On the front we drew landscapes of trees and flowers, with fluffy clouds, birds, a few dogs, cats, and rabbits. In the distance, great hills climbed toward the sun shining in one corner.

Hi, we wrote. *How are you?* I said I liked to read and draw. Anh said she liked to draw and listen to music. We wrote about fifth and sixth grade. We kept our sentences short and strict, as though our words would have to pass through censors. Inside her card Anh tucked a wallet-sized school picture. Unlike me, she looked fresh-faced and cute in her photos, her eyes never half shut in a blink. Searching for a semi-decent photo, I remembered that Mrs. Ryzema had taken a class picture of us fifth-graders sitting together in the school library. My smile wasn't as stiff as usual, nor my glasses and hair as askew. Rosa had been giving me Ogilvie home perms since my fourth-grade year, insisting that they would help me look pretty. The bleachy, dog-shampoo odor of the perm always seemed to fit the disappointment I felt each time she unwound the curlers. My hair never came close to the soft waves of the girl on the box, or the girls who tossed their heads sumptuously in the commercials for Prell, Finesse, and VO5. My straight black hair merely frizzed, sticking out at wayward angles. Rosa called it "natural-looking." I seized a pair of scissors and cut out my picture from the class portrait. My face ended up a polka dot in the palm of my hand, hardly bigger than an M&M. I dropped it into the card anyway. I didn't have Anh's face to show off, so it was probably better that our mother not know what I really looked like.

We handed our cards to Rosa, who said she would mail them. She looked them over, reading our messages, and I remembered how, when I was in first grade, she had intercepted a letter I had tried to send Jenny Adams. *Dear Jenny,* I had written. *I hate you. I hate you. I hate you.* Rosa had laid the open letter on the dining table in front of me and lectured me about being a mean and bad little girl.

I never found out if my mother got the cards. She doesn't remember. She didn't write back. For the first few weeks Anh and I waited in suspense and terror, as if everything we knew— our family, our house on Florence—might possibly break apart at the arrival of a response. The years of silence surrounding our mother had built within us a wall of fear: now that it had cracked, what else might? I half expected my father to react somehow—to talk to us. But he went about his business, working at the feather company, smoking at night, and watching television.

As the months passed without word, the subject of our mother seemed to slip back into the well of the unspoken. We went back to our regular lives. A year passed, then another. It was easy to go on. We had, after all, everything we had always known. We had a mother and a father, siblings, uncles, and Noi. The woman who had written from Pennsylvania remained a blank face, a gap on the page. How could we miss her if we did not know her?

After Crissy, Anh, Phuong, Vu, and I moved out and left for college, my parents began to change. By small degrees their voices softened; they asked not what grades we got but what classes we were taking. I chalked it up to living alone with Vinh and Noi. My father and Rosa had always looked after my brother with special care, perhaps because he was the only child equally theirs. He was, too, a mellower soul than the rest of us. Instead of hoarding toys and candy he shared them, wanting everyone to enjoy what he enjoyed. I decided he took after Noi—no other way to explain how our household had produced or sustained such a kind and mild creature. Perhaps he rubbed off on my parents, or perhaps the years of dealing with us girls had worn them down. Whenever I came home my father inquired if I had enough to eat. He made sure to supply me with plenty of my favorite Kung-Fu ramen, and he'd sauté an extra-large dinner of shrimp with scallions and garlic. "You want to eat something?" was his way of asking how I was doing. "You want McDonald's?" he'd ask. "Burger King? Pizza? Chinese food?"

The summer after my first year at the University of Michigan I took classes and worked at the front desk of a dormitory. My father and Rosa decided to go on a brief East Coast vacation with Anh and Vinh. They planned to see Boston and Cape Cod, then stop by Niagara Falls on the way back home.

Oh, yes, Rosa mentioned, they planned to visit my mother, too.

It had been eight years of silence since that letter from Swarthmore, Pennsylvania.

"Also," Rosa said, "your sister and brother." *Sister and brother?* I repeated. It took me a minute to figure out she didn't mean Anh and Vinh. Rosa didn't know how old this other sister and brother were, only that they had been born before Anh and me. "So," she said, cheerfully, as though she hadn't just dropped a thunderbolt, "we'll swing through Ann Arbor to pick you up." The matter-of-fact tone had resumed, a way to erase all the years since the letter.

When I told my supervisor that I needed a week off to go to Boston, he shook his head. Summer positions made no room for vacation time, he said. If I left I'd have to leave the job for good. He had a thicket of wavy blond hair and small steely eyes and wore leather jackets in eighty-degree weather. I remember how distraught he was when news reports announced Burt Reynolds and Loni Anderson's separation. "Not Burt and Loni!" he kept lamenting.

I called my father to tell him that I would lose my job if I went to Boston. "So what?" he said. "I'll give you some money." I waited for him, my stepmother, and sister to press me, convince me, tell me I was being ridiculous. *Quit your job now,* I wanted them to say. *We'll be in Ann Arbor in two weeks. You're coming with us.* But they didn't say anything more.

Had we been closer I wouldn't have hesitated to quit; I would have been comforted, sheltered by my family; I would have needed to be with them. But instead I felt the opposite. My parents might have softened a little, but it was too late, and not yet enough. I couldn't fathom meeting my mother with them. So they set off on their trip, me staying behind in Ann Arbor and nursing a strange feeling of regret and neglect. I told myself I needed to see my mother on my own, though the idea terrified me. Seeing her at all, in truth, terrified me, and I knew what I was really doing: avoiding, taking the coward's way into hiding.

A few weeks later I called Anh in East Lansing, where she went to MSU. We had been distant through most of our high school years and it would be a long while before we made up that lost time. We spoke like awkward colleagues. "How was it?" I asked vaguely.

"Okay," she said. "It was weird. It was fine."

The next summer, I met my mother.

She lived in Somerville, Massachusetts, and I had come to Boston to attend a wedding. We had agreed to meet in the lobby of a hotel in Newton, where I was staying. A few minutes before eleven in the morning, I saw them through the glass revolving doors: my half-sister and her husband. I went out to them in the broad summer sunlight.

When my mother's letter from Pennsylvania arrived in 1985 no one had mentioned the existence of a half-sister and a half-brother. But my parents had known all along, of course. Nho and Huy were several years older than Anh and I, and my father had met them way back when he was dating my mother in Saigon.

My half-sister Nho had long, permed hair and a broad face, as planed as mine but with sharper features. We smiled a lot, not quite looking at each other fully, as we walked to her burgundy Plymouth Horizon in the parking lot. In mostly unbroken silence her husband Binh, round, with a boyish smile, drove us to Somerville. They lived in a subsidized apartment complex—clusters of identically squat, bleak-looking brick buildings surrounded by parking lots. Two jungle gyms, clamped to the ground, highlighted the desolation.

I followed Nho and Binh to their apartment, passing through dim hallways that echoed our scuffles like an abandoned school. When we reached the door to their apartment it opened, and I knew the woman standing on the other side was my mother. We stood eye to eye. I could see in her face my sister Anh: softer features, blurred edges, a mushroom nose, a delicacy tempered by a strong, stubborn mouth. In size she was more like me: too short, the kind of person others called *tiny*. Except she was, at age forty-seven, pregnant for the last time. *She's six months,* Rosa had warned me over the phone right before I left, though the belly seemed hardly larger than a paunch.

She leaned forward and hugged me, a quick kiss hello as if we had only last seen each other a few months ago. "Look at you," she said, holding me at arm's length. She made a clicking noise with her tongue. "You're late. Almost twenty years I wait, and you're late."

She fluttered to the kitchen, insisting on pouring me an enormous plastic cup full of ice and Pepsi. Like Noi, she wore a tunic over flowy pants and soft slippers on her feet. But unlike Noi, whose silvery hair still fell to her knees when she unwound her bun each evening, my mother wore an obvious wig. It looked vaguely 1960s prom, too big for her head, and I wanted to ask her what had happened to all of her hair.

She lived with her boyfriend in a one-bedroom apartment upstairs but spent most of her time down here, with Nho, Binh, and their kids, Steven and Nancy, who were eight and six years old. They peered at me shyly, their eyes as wondering and mischievous as I imagined Anh and mine had been at their age. They shared a room with a red bunk bed. Like every corner of the apartment, the bedroom was crammed with household items: fans, cleaning supplies, folding chairs, stacks of blankets, towels, and clothes. In the living area a black leather sofa hunkered near an entertainment console decked out with a large TV, stereo system, and stacks of Vietnamese CDs. The pink window blinds over the windows were drawn, casting a dusky hue over the room.

We decided to all squeeze into the Plymouth and drive to Chinatown for dim sum. As Binh drove, switching between light rock and oldies stations on the radio, I looked out at the bright blue-skied day in Boston. The giant cranes of the Big Dig moved as if in time to the music in the car. My mother clasped my hand with hers. It was bony, the skin slippery. A solid jade bracelet enclosed her wrist. She would have to break it to remove it, or coax it off in a bath of warm water and soap.

"Agh," she sighed, "you should see how surprised I was when I came back and all of you—gone!" She spoke in such a deadpan manner that for a moment I thought she was joking.

"You just left. Poof! Gone. I'm so surprised." She lifted her hands and let them fall. "No note, no nothing. You all just suddenly left. And then I'm so sad."

I let out a small breath. "What did you do?"

"I cry," she said, still deadpan, as if delivering a punch line. "I cry for days and days."

As we walked through Chinatown, she told me that my father had sent her several packages when she lived in Saigon: aspirin, Band-Aids, toothbrushes and toothpaste, a little money. All that time he had known her address and she had known ours. Surely he had written her about Anh and me. How old we were getting. How well we were getting along in America. Maybe he told her how we couldn't get enough of Tom and Jerry cartoons, or Bert and Ernie on Sesame Street. My mother didn't remember. Only that, after a few years, the packages stopped coming.

In between relationships with Nho's father and my own father, she had had a brief affair with an American soldier in Saigon. He left long before she gave birth to their son, whom she named Huy. Years later, it would be Huy's status as a half-American child that would secure their entry into the United

States. After they arrived at the women's center in Pennsylvania in 1985, they found sponsors in Somerville, Massachusetts. My mother must have kept my father and Rosa updated on her whereabouts, for she said they had sent her a few checks over the years.

"I'm very thankful to them," she said quietly.

Throughout my childhood my father was someone I mostly tried to avoid. He was moody, with an unpredictable temper, and nobody wanted to be in range when he got angry. But sometimes, when he had too much drink on Christmas Day, he would get sentimental and start talking about Vietnam. I seized these chances to ask how we had left in 1975. I even couched the question in safe terms: it was for a school report. My father told the story a little differently each time—hours shifted; the cook on the ship might morph into the captain. Once he said we went all the way to the airport before deciding we would have better luck getting out by boat. There were only two occasions when I felt brave enough, and my father seemed jovial enough—the drunkenness at that safe area before he became belligerent—to ask what happened to my mother. The first time, my father said she was with us. Then a bomb went off and she panicked, got lost in the crowd, and we had to get on the ship without her. The second time, he said she was stuck at her mother's house across the river, that the bridges to our house had been bombed or guards had refused to let people cross. When my father told these stories a stern look settled over his face and I knew not to pursue the questions. I understood why we had left her behind—we knew a lot of families in similar situations, with relatives stranded in Vietnam, waiting for sponsorship papers—but I wanted to know what it had been like, being him, making that choice. I wanted to know what thoughts had flown through his mind. Guilt, sorrow?

How often did he think about that night? Did he miss her? Did he love her?

This is what my mother said:

The week before April 29, Anh had been staying with her and Nho and Huy at her mother's house. But Anh wouldn't stop crying and whining—she wanted bananas, and no one had any. Frustrated, my mother brought Anh to Noi's place across the river, where Noi had been taking care of me. My mother had no idea what lay ahead, that it would be nearly twenty years before she would see us again. She knew that almost everyone in Saigon was talking about leaving, but she thought it was just talk. Rumors, not plans. Days later we were running toward a ship at the harbor while she was at home, waiting out the shelling, hoping her neighborhood would be spared.

A few days after the official surrender she thought it would be safe enough to go back to Noi's house. She found the place empty, the furniture, cooking pans, everything taken away by neighbors and looters. Outside, the man who lived next door told her—*eh, didn't you know?*—we had left for America. He urged her to check if we had left a note. But she had already searched every crevice. She started walking back home, slowly, looking back just in case she'd spot us there after all. The neighbor repeated his information that we had fled the country, calling it after her. There was nothing left for her to do but return to her mother's house and wait.

At the China Pearl, sassy old waitresses pushed their dim sum carts around the tables, calling out the names of dishes in a bored tone. The restaurant had two stories full of packed family tables at peak brunch hour. Puffs of steam rose every time a waitress lifted the lid of a steaming basket of dumplings. Nho and Binh took charge, scooping up several plates of shrimp rice rolls, Nancy and Steven's favorite dish. They loved to watch the waitress pour a squiggle of soy sauce on the wide, flat noodles that threatened to slip from their chopsticks. I hadn't eaten dim sum since my family had taken a summer trip to Toronto and Niagara Falls more than ten years ago. I remembered how we had all boarded the *Maid of the Mist* to see the falls up close, the spray hitting us full in the face. In Toronto, my father had thrown a fit when my sisters and I begged him to let us ride the elevator to the top of the CN Tower. He had a fear of heights, and if he wouldn't go up there, then none of us would. Then we went to a dim sum restaurant somewhere in Chinatown. I remember my astonishment at having the choices rolled right by us, on display, there for the taking. My father and Noi made all of the selections, mindful of how each plate added up when the waitress stamped the bill on our table. I remember how much my father loved the steamed chicken feet, which none of us kids would taste, and how Noi slipped morsels of shrimp dumpling, blushing pink and expertly halved, onto my plate. Before heading home, we stopped at an Asian market and loaded up on produce that was hard to get in Grand Rapids—soursop, guava, green papaya. Rosa covered the boxes of fruit with our jackets, hiding them on the floor of the backseat, and when we got close to customs control at the border she ordered us to pretend to be asleep.

I didn't speak of any of this at the China Pearl, where our table filled up with tin and bamboo steamers of shrimp *shumai*, the bright green of chives and scallions translucent through the delicate skins. We ate spareribs, shrimp balls, and sticky buns stuffed with red pork. We reached for barbecue pork buns, lotus seed buns, sesame balls, beef meatballs, more shrimp, and parfait cups containing Jell-O cubes and melon balls with paper umbrellas perched on top. Nho, Binh, and my mother kept the food coming, anxious to show their welcome through generosity. It was just what Noi would have done, I knew.

We didn't talk much, letting the noise of the restaurant—the clatter of tin baskets, the sharp calls of the waitresses, families seeming to shout as they talked—float between our conversation about Nancy and Steven and how they liked school. Almost every Asian family I had ever seen didn't know how to distinguish between talking and shouting. But we kept quiet, not yet knowing what to say to each other. Every once in a while Nancy, who had the same button-nose I'd had at her age, and almost the same bowl haircut, threw me an impish smile. She didn't look like a Nancy to me; it was such a severe, non-Vietnamese name.

I asked my mother about her baby. "It's a girl," she said, patting the green shimmering polyester covering her abdomen.

Five children. It was strange to think of that number, when all my life I had assumed she had had only Anh and me. It was almost a retroactive comfort to know otherwise, and to think that she had not been so alone in Vietnam.

Our meal was done. Napkins stained with soy sauce, the table littered with empty teacups, dishes, and tin steamer pans. All around us Asian languages gathered and swelled. We rose and traveled in a body down the stairs and toward the exit. Out into the summer heat we started walking, passing butchers with glorious red-shellacked ducks hanging in the windows and clothing stores bursting with bolts of silk.

We stopped at a storefront display of watches, scarves, and rhinestone jewelry. "I buy you something," my mother declared, already pushing toward the entrance.

I protested, unable to bear the idea of her spending what little money she had on me. "Let's buy something for the baby later on," I said.

We found ourselves in the shop next door, a neon-lit bakery filled with dozens of varieties of bean cakes, rice cakes, and butter cookies behind slanted glass cases. A row of cream cakes—white genoise layered with fresh strawberries and fruit and covered with whipped cream—called out to us with their unmarred surfaces. I was drawn to a shelf of mooncakes pressed into different shapes: a dragon, a dollar sign, and Buddha. It was the fat happy Buddha, his face scrunched up in laughter. A map of his body in golden dough relief. Before I knew it my mother had ordered and paid for one. She put the cake in my hands. Buddha, wrapped in wax paper and tucked in a brown slip of a bag, felt heavier than I expected. The moon cake's thick outer crust protected a solid filling of green mung bean paste. I knew its pasty texture and sweet, dusty smell. At home, mooncakes always came around during Tet. I didn't care much for the flavor or feel of bean paste, but I could never resist taking one bite to see if I had changed my mind. The taste lingered, making my mouth feel dry. I preferred the sweetness of candy and caramelized sugar. I always wanted mooncakes to be something other than they were.

I carried that Buddha-shaped mooncake all over Chinatown. Every time I glanced at a shop window my mother offered to buy whatever I saw there. Watches, shoes, all manner of gold and jade jewelry. Her offers filled me with guilt and the fleeting wish to be a little girl again so I could accept her gifts and so erase all the years that divided us.

Nancy and Steven, walking ahead with Nho and Binh, glanced back at us with small, curious smiles. They held their parents' hands. Huy, my half-brother, the half-American, was supposed to meet us at the restaurant but had never shown up. I had a hundred questions to ask my mother. I wanted to know what it had been like to arrive in Boston, how they had gotten along those first unfamiliar weeks. Nho had been twenty years old then, Huy sixteen. My mother worked where she works still, at a small office products factory just a few miles from her apartment. She fills envelope boxes with their envelopes, sitting in a line of other women not unlike her—a little older, a little weary, but eager for company, gossip, and any reason to laugh. I wanted to know how she had met my father, and what kind of relationship they had had. I wanted to know when I was born and if she remembered the time of day or night. I wondered what she had thought about when she looked at me and Anh. Two more children. Two more girls.

Suddenly my mother said, "Rosa—she a good mother." I couldn't tell if it was a question or a declaration. So I said, "Yes."

"She good," my mother repeated. There was no trace of sadness in her voice. "A very, very good lady. She good mother for you."

"Yes," I agreed. *I'm very thankful,* she had said earlier, and it finally dawned on me that she was thankful not for the money my parents sent but for the fact that they had raised me and Anh.

They had taken care of us. Oh, we desired a million selfish things, but we had never really gone without. We were the fortunate ones. That's what my mother was pressing on me—what I hadn't ever fully seen.

The afternoon sun poured down, unfiltered by clouds. It was getting time for me to get back to the hotel so I could attend the wedding of two people I'd never see again. It seemed ages ago since I had been anywhere but here, walking slowly through Boston with my mother. So many questions, yet no voice and no time. What was I afraid of? Of starting to talk and being unable to stop? I looked in every store window, all the arrangements of sequined purses and fake flowers, to find the answer to what I was supposed to feel.

I remained a stranger or a ghost, something in between. Binh weaved expertly through traffic on the way to Newton, while in the backseat I struggled for conversation. In the end, I left without my mother ever knowing where I lived, or how I had chosen my apartment in Ann Arbor because it was located on Ingalls Street. She didn't know my major, or the hours I spent combing through the library stacks to find obscure research for my English papers. I didn't know how to describe these things. Our conversations were rudimentary. *Do you like school? Yes. Do you get good grades? Yes. That's good.* And then me saying: *Do you like Boston? Yes. Me, too.* It was as though we were practicing language conversations out of a workbook.

In the end, I realized that I had never had fantasies of meeting my mother. On soap operas I had seen people reuniting with great cries and splashing tears. They would run at each other at full speed across a giant meadow or parking lot or airport. I never imagined this for myself. Nothing about my mother spoke to my idea of fantasy. To me, growing up in Grand Rapids, fantasy meant ruffled canopy beds, pink teddy bears, a plate of home-made chocolate chip cookies sitting on a desk beside a new pile of books. I had always known that whoever my mother was, she was not the stuff of fantasies. She was, on the contrary, the stuff of too much reality. And I had avoided that reality—my whole family had—for years. In the end, I realized how easy it had been for my father and Rosa to stay silent, to keep the walls of our family boundaries intact.

In the hypothetical, you think of how much you will have to say, how the questions will just flow and flow, trying to cover the years of separation. You think all you'll want to do is get to know the mother you have never met. But in the end you are left with an oil-stained bag containing a Buddha-shaped mooncake. I am left with that cake. And I could not eat it. I carried it back to my hotel and stuffed it into my suitcase. I brought it back to my Ann Arbor apartment before finally throwing it into the trash. Buddha's face had smudged against the paper, blurred with grease.

Two months later, Anh and I decided to send a gift of baby clothes to our mother. In the backs of our minds we awaited word of our new sister's arrival, but no news came. That Thanksgiving in Grand Rapids, I mentioned this to my father and step-mother. Though we had become a little more open with each other by then, less afraid to face the complications of our family, I was glad that they had never asked me about meeting my mother in Boston. *Oh,* Rosa said in a no-nonsense voice, *she lost the baby.* She had gone into premature labor in her seventh month, and the baby was dead before Anh and I had ever mailed her the clothes we had picked out from Baby Gap. It was just one of the things my parents shelved and didn't get around to telling us.

It was early May in Saigon, 1975, a few days after the city's fall, when my mother returned to the house where my father, Anh, and I had lived with Noi. I imagined her opening the door and feeling, instantly, the emptiness. The smell of it—notes of incense and jasmine tea. She stumbled back out in the narrow street. A man sitting in his doorway called out to her. *They're gone. They went to America.* She didn't believe him. *Maybe they left you a note,* he said. He was bored; the whole day lay in front of him. She went back into the house to look again for the note that wasn't there. She got down on her knees to examine the floor, but found only dust. She left our house slowly, the shock so clear on her face that the neighbor leaned forward to repeat the news to her—*They're gone*—as if she were hard of hearing. *They went to America.*

In the end, I left my questions unanswered. I couldn't comprehend the loss, the nearly twenty years' absence, the silence and unknowing, the physical distance literally impossible to break. I didn't know what to say to make anything different. I didn't know what to do with so many years between us. In the end, my mother and her family drove me to the hotel in Newton, Massachusetts. I got out of the car. We hugged our good-byes. My mother assessed me up and down, as she had a few hours earlier, and pronounced me too skinny in the way that Vietnamese women do. When she touched me I felt the cool of her jade bracelet on my skin. They walked me to the door of the hotel and let me go, waiting until I had pushed beyond the revolving door into the lobby. I turned to see them once more—my half-sister and her husband, my niece and nephew, and my mother. They waved and smiled as if I were going down the jetway to an airplane and a long, long flight out of there. I walked to the bank of elevators. In the end, I left my mother all over again.

16

Cha Gio

I WENT TO VIETNAM WITH NOI AND MY UNCLE CHU Anh in the spring of 1997. My father wouldn't go because he was afraid of flying. "If you don't get on a plane you'll never get to see Vietnam again," I said, stating the obvious. "Oh, I don't know," he replied in an offhand way, which meant that he didn't care to discuss it. I had originally planned to go by myself—I had received a grad school travel grant—but when my father recruited his sensible brother to look out for me, I realized that I didn't want to go to Vietnam without Noi. We made a plan to start in Saigon and work our way north to Hanoi. There, Noi would be able to reunite with her siblings whom she hadn't seen since 1954.

The moment we arrived in Saigon, bleary and dazed after nearly twenty-four hours of travel, we encountered the fierce heat that would press on us for the next four weeks. It was May, and the air was thick with the humidity of the incipient rainy season. Just outside the airport, a throng of people waited for arrivals among cabdrivers smoking and honking their horns at nobody in particular. Then a small band of men and women—cousins, great-aunts and great-uncles my father had contacted—pushed forward to claim us. The women, dressed in bright *ao dai*s, waved stalks of gladioli at us as they swept us into a cab.

They lived in a neighborhood of muddied alleys, in a concrete home with a red-tiled roof, on the outskirts of Saigon. As guests, our duty was to sit on the hardwood sofa, sip jasmine tea, and nibble Pirouline wafers and fruit. Someone poured me a tall glass of 7UP with a slab of ice. I ate a piece of pineapple so sweet that I gasped.

I had no way to keep up with the frenzied pace at which Noi, Chu Anh, and my relatives were talking, so I just gazed around the room. I longed to explore the house, especially since I was certain I could hear pigs and roosters in the yard, and several cats wandered in and out at leisure. In the living room, the dark wood altar to the ancestors was a lot like Noi's at home, with a statue of Buddha presiding above all. Nearby, a television broadcast a Vietnamese soap opera. The cement floor had a long hairline fracture that led to a mahogany bed shielded by a bamboo screen. The windows had bars over them instead of glass, and the wide front door, like most I saw in neighborhoods in Saigon, lay open to passersby.

That first afternoon in Vietnam, a cat died while I was looking at it. She was bovine-looking, white with black spots, dozing under my second cousin's chair. After a while I realized that she was lying in an unusually still way. Curious, I got out of my seat and touched the cat with one finger. *"Con meo chet roi,"* I said without thinking. *The cat just died.* My cousin laughed and said that the cat was just lazy and slept a lot. Noi, from her spot on the sofa, looked at the cat and furrowed her brow. *"Chet cha,"* she exclaimed.

For days the dead cat unnerved me. One moment alive,

sleeping like any ordinary cat—the next moment gone. She had passed from one form to another in front of my eyes. I thought of reincarnation, of ghosts hovering all around us. I wondered where the spirit of the cat would go.

The next few days we stayed with another relative who lived in a spacious two-story home in a busy urban area closer to down-town. Co Nga had a well-paying job at a bank, and even had an air-conditioning unit in one room on the second floor. That's where she insisted Noi and I sleep, and we gratefully accepted. After the heat of the days visiting Buddhist temples, calling on old friends and relatives, and walking around downtown, we were glad to lie on the twin beds and breathe cool air.

On my first night at Co Nga's I stood for ten minutes in front of her house wondering how I could possibly cross the street to check out the shoe store on the other side. The flow of mopeds, cars, and bicyclists never waned and never stopped beeping. There were men bearing impossible bundles with their bicycles—stacks of ice, long pieces of plastic pipe, a huge turtle floating in a fish tank. After a while, a little boy approached me and told me he'd help me cross. He was maybe seven or eight years old, but when he took my hand and led me into the path of the oncoming traf-fic, I followed him. We moved steadily across the street, pausing and meandering as the motorcycles bent to make room for us.

In the mornings Co Nga served us bowls of *pho* redolent with star anise and heaped with bean sprouts and herbs. She set out plates of mangosteen, branches of lychee and longan fruit, and sliced watermelon. I loved to strip away the pebbled skin of a ly-chee and pop the translucent eyeball into my mouth, sucking the flesh away from the varnished pit. I couldn't get enough of the crunchy, cold watermelon; it tasted sweeter and deeper—more thoroughly watermelon—than any I had ever tasted in America. In the evenings Co Nga steamed enormous shrimp with their heads on and stewed fish in spicy sauces with coriander, chilies, and *nuoc mam*. She sautéed slices of beef with lemongrass and vegetables and cooked up a pungent *canh chua* fish soup with tomatoes. Worried that I would only like American food, she also made a heap of broad-cut french fries every night.

A few years back Co Nga had taken in an old, dying uncle. She fed and washed him, helped him up and down from the little bed near the kitchen where he slept all day. He was ancient, with a long wispy beard, and he had lost most of his vision. When he sat at the table he didn't appear to be aware of us at all. Co Nga cooked him a watery rice porridge—*chao*, something Noi always made for me when I was sick—and I couldn't help watching him eat it. He leaned into the bowl, dragging his beard along the surface of the gruel as he took great sloppy slurps. Two or three times a meal he would pause to release a huge slow-motion sneeze.

One day in Saigon, Noi, Chu Anh, and I visited the house where we had lived up until April 29, 1975. The cab dropped us off at the entrance to one of the city's many neighborhood mazes of concrete walls divided into houses. The narrow road twisted back and forth, and Noi said that it would lead eventually to the temple she had walked to almost every day. On Sundays, she had gone to a bigger, grander temple nearby.

Our house was anonymous-looking, just a square of space separated into rooms. The man who lived there now invited us in to look around. He appeared to be a bachelor, with old towels and blankets draped over a worn wooden sofabed. The television was tuned to a soccer match. I stood in the dim light, taking in the cement walls, the cooking pots and hot plate in one corner, the curtain in front of the bedroom. Noi pointed to a corner and said something about a desk full of papers and pictures that had once been there. She recalled the day a calendar had jumped off the wall and she knew it was another sign from her son Quan. He had often spoken to her here.

Chu Anh walked around, shaking his head. "I can't believe we lived like this," he said. In Atlanta, where he works as an engineer, he drives home to a quiet house in a named subdivision.

I tried to imagine the years my father and uncles and grandmother spent here, having no idea that they would one day flee it, leaving everything behind. I tried to picture the stories my father and uncles had told me. Was this where the cat with the pet rat slept on languid afternoons? Where did the angry chicken hang out? I tried to imagine my sister and me, so little and so demanding—my sister's feet stamping the concrete floor, Noi feeding us mashed bananas as she contemplated our future. The dingy, gray rooms held no resonance for me, no meaning. This home was not my home to remember.

Walking back to the cab, we passed a gaggle of boys lounging in a grotto. They were playing cards and smoking, and they eyed us with curiosity. Above them hung an old magazine picture of Elizabeth Taylor as Maggie the Cat. It was only then that I could see my father here—I could see him in these boys' faces. I could see him burning his moped down the alleyways, taking the turns too sharply, maybe racing somewhere to see my mother.

I went there the next day, to see my mother's mother—my other grandmother, my *ngoai*. She lived across the river in an outlying district of Saigon, where cars stirred up clouds of red dust. Her house occupied a square in a row of barracks facing identical rows, all of the doors opened to the air. As I walked down the dirt lane, peering at the faded numbers etched near the doorways, an old woman pushed a food cart past me, crying out, *Chicken!* to the mostly empty road.

My grandmother *ngoai* lived with one of my aunts, who looked like a rounder, plumper version of my mother. Hammered gold bracelets jangled on her arms as she reached out to take hold of me. Her daughter—one of my cousins—was maybe four years old and amused herself by sticking her head into the sack of rice sitting in the corner of the kitchen. "You are an American girl," my aunt said to me in Vietnamese, with teasing and pride in her voice. She sat me down in the living room, facing the altar to the ancestors, and brought out glasses of Coke, cups of jasmine tea, freshly fried shrimp chips, and a tray of soursop and lychees. From her end of the sofa, my grandmother lifted her head toward me. A frail, bony creature with thick glasses and a broad, flattened mouth, she was only a few years older than Noi but looked almost as ancient as Co Nga's uncle. She reached out a gnarled, shiny hand and laid it on mine. She said my name out loud and smiled, exposing a maroon-red mouth. For a moment I panicked, thinking it was blood, until I realized that it was the stain of the betel nut she chewed.

She and my aunt knew almost no English and I knew only rudimentary Vietnamese so we couldn't say much. I had come too late in the morning, and the sun was getting too intense, the dust rising. So we spent an hour just looking at each other, and smiling, and I drank too much Coke just to have something to do.

Before the trip I had felt ready to go, secure with my travel grant money, but now I think I could never have been ready. I could not have prepared myself for the feeling of being a tourist in the country where I was supposed to have grown up, of being a foreigner among people who were supposed to be mine. Every girl I passed on the street was my theoretical double, a person I might have been, a life I might have had. Sitting with my aunt and grandmother, I did not feel a rush of love. I felt regret, exhaustion. I felt like an outsider, and I knew I would always be just that. I would fly back home to the United States and perhaps never see them again.

Before I left I slipped them an envelope full of American money, as my uncle and I had discussed. Still, I walked away from their house feeling a profound sense of failure. I did not want to imagine years of deprivation and wondering, my mother staring out the window season after season, finding imaginary shapes in the red earth. I didn't know how to think of her walking home, her whole body shaking with grief. How long she must have waited to get word on our whereabouts. How many times she must have imagined our growing up—she had known me for only eight months, my sister only two years. How did she picture us, becoming American as TV, changing into people beyond her recognition?

When I think of my childhood I think of contrasts: the melting chocolate of a Mr. Goodbar against the cool crumble of Swee-Tarts. I think of drifts of snow reaching the windows, then green summer days casting out beyond Jennifer Vander Wal's back-yard. I think of my father standing outside smoking, a skinny, solitary figure in his beige sweater with brown stripes; I think of him coming home with pockets full of candy and gum. I think of the mother I didn't know walking down a sunburnt lane in Saigon while my stepmother drove her black Ford Tempo through Grand Rapids to get to work. I think of my face in the mirror, flat and sallow, wishing to become the same as all the beautiful, bright-eyed girls in my books and school.

In the fall, leaves crackled as I walked to Ken-O-Sha Elementary, the days growing shorter and colder. In the winter, Noi's jasmine tea fragranced the air. I looked into the amber liquid to read the leaves scattered at the bottom of the cup. Noi's knitting needles flashed as she created cardigans out of intricate stitch patterns and cables. Then warm weather would seep back— the spring giving way grudgingly, often making us wear jackets well into May—and I would return to long afternoons plotting out my next episodes of candy, ice cream, and fruit. In the summer, we ate chilled globes of canned lychee from china cups. We slept in the basement to escape the upstairs heat, jumping heedlessly on my uncles' Eames lounges and feeling, for brief moments, thrilled to be alive, kids, with all the MTV we could want. Sometimes, a tornado siren would blare through the neighborhood and my father would go out to see the storm. I would creep back upstairs, too curious not to look, and always would be surprised by the stillness of the air, the yellowness of the sky. I had nightmares of funnel clouds aiming right at us. But somehow, in real life, they missed us even as my father waited on the front porch with a glass of cognac in his hand. *Why don't you go to the basement?* I asked him once. *Because I have to protect,* he said.

After a good rain, toadstools would crop up all over the yard on Florence Street and Noi would pull up each one. I think she must have pictured my sister and me stealing away with them,

putting that foreign substance in our mouths. She never acknowledged the neighborhood children when they laughed at her squat-
ting in the yard, their cheeks puffed with derision. She pulled up
the toadstools to save us.

When I think of Grand Rapids I think of how much time I
spent trying to make real the dream of the blond-haired girl with
a Betty Crocker mother and a kitchen to match. Cocooned in
my own silence, I dreamed of the day when I would be a grown-
up at last. Then, I thought, I could eat whipped cream and SpaghettiOs every day and say whatever I wanted. Spurning my own
reflection for what it could never give me, I thought I could make
myself over from the inside out.

In truth, everything that was real lay right in front of me:
oranges after dinner; pomegranates in winter; mangoes cubed off
their skin. Birthday cakes decorated in my own hand while my
stepmother taught me the words to *"Cumpleaños feliz."* We had
sopa and rice, sloppy Joes and fast food, curries and stew, soups
and stir-fries, noodles and ramen, steak and french fries. Even on
the nights Rosa made dinner, Noi cooked for my uncles and the
ancestors. She had the rice cooker going before we came home
from school, so we could eat something right away if we were
hungry. And when I scorned her food, reaching for Jays potato
chips or Little Debbie snack cakes, she did not scold my wayward
desires. She knew I would return, night after night, asking permission to go to sleep. I returned to her in meditation, trying to
keep my back straight, trying to stop the erosion of language I
myself had started. I returned to her when I woke early in the
morning to the sound of her wooden mallet grinding shrimp and
pork for *cha gio.*

I've watched her countless times rolling them out for a party or for Tet. She sat on the dining room floor, mixing the ingredients with her hands. She grated a mound of carrots, her fingers flying. She knew just how much fish sauce and black pepper and mung bean noodles to use. When the mixture was ready I tried to help shape some *cha gio:* a forkful of the filling on a triangle of *banh trang* spring roll wrapper; the left and right corners folded in; a quick roll and it all came together, smooth and slim, sealed with a dab of egg yolk. When I formed *cha gio* that were lumpy and bloated Noi laughed, unrolled them, and showed me again. Later, I would watch Noi pluck the *cha gio* from the frying pan and lay them in a cloth-lined colander. I could count on the first anticipated bite, the sweet and peppery flavors of shrimp and pork and fish sauce weighed against the delicate crunch of the fried wrapper. In the middle of the night I would eat the leftovers cold, by the light of the open refrigerator door. They tasted even sweeter then, the texture of wood-ears and noodles more distinct; I ate slowly, trying to memorize the flavors, trying to know what my grandmother has always known: this amount of pepper, that amount of fish sauce. She had always been there to show me this world without measurements.

My father and Rosa remarried each other fifteen years after their first wedding, in the same Grand Rapids courthouse. They had both stayed on in the Ada house after the divorce, amicably enough to keep Thanksgivings and Christmas holidays their usual mix of food-gorging, boredom, and unanchored tension. No wonder we always kept the TV at top volume, playing a parade of action-adventure movies. Possibly it had taken a nearly empty house, save for Vinh, for my parents to reach their détente.

Each year now they renovate another part of the house—a wall torn down or replaced, old carpet changed to tile. They purchase huge statues of Buddhas and goddesses, some as tall as six feet. The female Buddha, with her regal, painted dress, governs the front of the house. My father swears that she's become a good luck shrine, and that total strangers will stop by to pay their respects to her. At night, my father and Rosa often sleep on different ends of the same sofa sectional, their feet meeting at right angles to each other. The TV will keep blaring. All the land around the house has been built up with office buildings, but they refuse to leave their tucked-away plot where the willow branches fall away with each summer storm. They even refuse to install air-conditioning, swearing that the swimming pool is good enough. When we first moved in, the ceiling of the swimming pool room had been unfinished—just exposed beams and insulation—and my father resolved to finish the job. Balancing on home-built scaffolding, he pieced together rows of cedar planks. I remember how peaceful he seemed, working alone. Later, in the snowy months of the year, Noi would jog lightly around the pool for exercise. Under the blue tarp, the water grew moldy and green.

The last foster brothers who stayed with us, Pina and Thien, had loved that swimming pool. They were from Cambodia, where they had lost two parents and a brother. Pina had a gentle manner and a quick, brilliant smile; people who knew him for five minutes remembered him forever. He and Thien called Rosa *Mom* but they hardly knew us. They stayed with us only a few months. Thien ran off, then Pina went after him. They ended up in California, we heard, but that was the last we knew of them for years.

So many mysteries floating through our household; so much chaos and silence, intertwined.

Back home for the holidays, my family gathers around platters of *cha gio*, fried shrimp, shrimp *à la plancha*, and *goi cuon*. We eat in the living room, where everyone is already drinking too much. "Have some more wines," my father urges, holding out a bottle of red. I go help Noi in the kitchen, wondering how many *cha gio*, in a lifetime of *cha gio*, she has monitored with her chopsticks. She lives now with Chu Cuong, his wife, and their ten-year-old son, Anthony, taking care of him as she took care of my siblings and me.

The next day we will drive into southeastern Grand Rapids for dim sum, and I will be astonished by how much the city has changed: there are white people in the Vietnamese markets, white people eating bean curd and *banh bao*. The way to Florence Street is filled with new strip malls and subdivisions. The last time we saw the old house the orange door in the dining room wall was still there, unmet by a deck, unusable. I hope it stays that way, as much a signpost as a pair of yellow pants in a crowd.

When I think of Grand Rapids, I think of bitter winter days standing at the bus stop, shouting Air Supply songs into the clouds. I think of sitting in the plum tree with Jennifer Vander Wal, arguing about the existence of God. I think of my short family walking among the tall blonds of western Michigan, standing on tiptoes to see as much as we could.

I think of a letter I never read, postmarked in Swarthmore, Pennsylvania.

I think of Noi's blue bedrooms, and the calm I always felt

when I walked by the statue of Buddha. Eyeing the plums and peaches heaped on the altar, I closed my eyes to give my respect to him, to the ancestors, and to the spirits of all our dead relatives.

I think of the magic held in a piece of fruit, a Bosc pear opened into luminous crescent moons. Noi and I would sit cross-legged while I did homework, watched TV, and worked on Noi's puzzle all at the same time. She murmured a little *oomph* of approval when one of us set a piece into place, admiring the perfection of the fit. Together we created landscapes of places neither of us knew: flower-filled meadows in Switzerland, vistas of the Rocky Mountains. The nights never felt cold or unwelcoming in Noi's room, no matter how much snow accumulated outside.

I think of escape—a last-minute decision, night in a falling city, a departure without a single message left behind. What it must have been for my father, taking Anh and me into his arms, pursuing a boat, a way out, knowing all the while that our mother would not know where we were. Perhaps he told himself that she might leave, too, or that we would be able to send for her. Perhaps he steeled himself to a choice that would never have been made differently: his children, their future, their lives came first. That I cannot imagine that moment, the panic and fear, the push to leave his country and aim for an unknown land, is perhaps his gift. It is my Americanness. What my father must have thought, what must have replayed in his mind for years—I cannot ever really grasp. In just a few minutes, in half a night, our lives changed. Our identities changed. We were Vietnamese, we were refugees, we were Americans. My father could not possibly regret it. I do not regret it. I am grateful for his unimaginable choice.

On a hill in a cemetery just outside Hanoi, my grandmother stood with her sisters at the spot where their parents' ashes were buried. They're matriarchs in this matrilineal country, the ones who survived and endured. I watched them from a distance, admiring the way they all held their umbrellas just so, their elbows bent in the exact same way, to create a scrim between their bodies and the sun. Noi's sisters couldn't stop marveling at how old Noi had gotten, and she couldn't stop marveling at them. They giggled and shouted about it all the way back to the youngest sister's house, where a feast awaited us: crepes stuffed with vegetables, fish heads and herbs floating in sweet and sour broth, beef stewed with eggs, shrimp dipped in *nuoc mam* spiked with lime and pepper, chicken tossed with cellophane noodles, fresh spring rolls bursting with bean sprouts, shrimp, and coriander, and always, for the American girl, a plate of fresh french fries. We sat in a circle on the floor, spreading the dishes out in front of us between our rice bowls and glasses of 7UP and Tiger beer.

I think of riding a train all through the night to the coast of Nha Trang. I stood at the open window just outside the compartment that Noi, Chu Anh, and I shared, sticking my head out a little to feel the breeze. I thought I could never look enough at the moonlight and how it skimmed the top of the rice paddies. Every hour or so the train would stop for no apparent reason, and it was then I could see stilted huts and, toward sunrise, the glow of cooking fires, the dim figures of women in conical hats working in the fields.

In Hanoi, I stood near the great Hoan Kiem Lake while the fire-orange blossoms of a *phuong vy* tree fluttered down on me. I tilted my head back to feel the tear-shaped petals on my face. They blurred as they fell, a vibrancy that not even the rain could tame. I picked up a few and sat on a bench to press them into the journal I had brought. I had scarcely written in it, having few words to convey where I was, this Vietnamese-born American girl returning for a visit. As I sat there, trying to press the color into the page and into my mind, memorizing the grace and strength of the thin branches, an elderly woman approached me. She had been watching, and she held out her hand to offer a few petals she had plucked. I thanked her in Vietnamese. *Cam on ba.* The woman wore a buttoned tunic over light cotton pants and carried a grocery bag. I watched her walk the path around this lake where, I had learned, a legendary turtle had once reclaimed a magic sword from an emperor. People say such a turtle still haunts the waters, and that whoever sees him will find good fortune. There are those who sit at the lake every day, waiting for the vision to rise from the early morning mist.

Author's Note

I THINK OF THIS MEMOIR AS AN HOMAGE TO CHILD-hood, suburbia, and all the bad food, fashion, music, and hair of the deep 1980s. It is also about an immigrant's dilemma to blend in or remain apart. This anxiety, which so many of my memories involve, became the logical grounding for the whole book. It required writing about tensions and conflicts, family and friends, literal and imagined homes—the moments that led me to figure out what kind of identity I wanted to have. A few other decisions I made in writing this memoir include: changing some people's names and identifying information; sticking to certain thematic frameworks, even if it meant cutting long paragraphs devoted to the bands Supertramp, Toto, and Styx; and owning up to my memories rather than others'. Although I did need to rely on stories from my father, uncles, and grandmother to depict our escape from Saigon, I generally tried to avoid turning my family into collaborators. The book, after all, can only represent the views of the author. I do not mean to speak for all of my family, or all Vietnamese immigrants, many of whom have had entirely different experiences with, and opinions on, assimilation, culture, and language. If memory is a shifting mirror, then writing is an effort to keep it stilled, if only for a while, to try to find a point of focus, some sense of understanding. This book is my articulation of memories and experiences as I believe them—call it one person's perspective on being Vietnamese and American, and on being a kid in America, growing up with all the wants, frustrations, and bright-colored packaging that make up the landscape of childhood.

Acknowledgments

Several brief passages in this book were adapted from essays previously published as: "A World Without Measurements" (*Gourmet* magazine); "Toadstools" (*Dream Me Home Safely*); and "The Good Immigrant Student" (*Tales Out of School*).

Many, many thanks to Molly Stern for her invaluable guidance, and to Laura Tisdel, Alessandra Lusardi, Kate Griggs, and Sonya Cheuse. I am grateful also to the wonderful Tim Seldes.

I thank the PEN American Center and the judges who selected *Stealing Buddha's Dinner* to receive the PEN/Jerard Fund Award. Thanks also the the University of Michigan and Purdue University for their past and present support.

I am deeply grateful to all of my family: for taking chances, for putting up with me, for feeding me well, and for being their own true selves.

Finally, I thank my husband, Porter Shreve. His constant support, encouragement, and infallible critiques helped me figure out what I really wanted, and needed, to write.

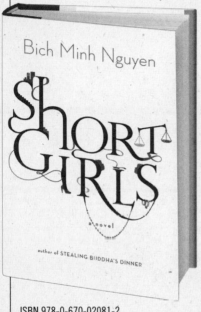